You Must Be Tired

by

Pat Farr

1997

Dedicated to

Cdr. Mike Farr R.N. OBE

1939 - 2000

Table of Contents

Preface

In order to have a pool of interpreters, the Armed Services used to take it in turns to send an Officer to Hong Kong to learn Chinese. Mike had volunteered when it was the turn of the Royal Navy: less because of a burning desire to study, more that it meant living in Hong Kong where he had a girlfriend. To his surprise, he was chosen but, also to his surprise, upon his arrival his girlfriend announced that she was getting married the following week – to someone else!

Roll on a few years: there was increased interest from the Chinese Navy in the possible purchase of equipment and technology from the West, and the British Defence Attaché requested a Naval Attaché be appointed, as he was 'out of his depth' with things maritime. Someone was chosen whose Chinese was both fluent and expert. Mike's was decidedly rusty from years of non use. Then, quite unexpectedly, the designated Officer decided that he was changing direction and would be doing missionary work. Plan B: Mike was to be the Naval Attaché!

We had just moved into a new area, and new Navy housing: as I happily announced that the last box was unpacked and the last picture hung, Mike said the immortal words "It's all been changed". He was to leave very soon for Attaché training and then a refresher course in Chinese, whilst I juggled two small children, re-homing cats and dogs and repacking!

The following narrative, written in 1997, are my recollections of two amazing tours of duty in Beijing: 1981-3 and 1986-90.

Chapter One: This Is China

My first impression of The People's Republic of China was grey and cold – very grey and very cold! Admittedly it was February and we had just spent three weeks in Hong Kong where it was so hot (compared with Scotland) that we had had to buy ourselves summer clothes and sun cream, but the stark Arrivals Hall with po-faced armed soldiers and a mere smattering of 40 watt light bulbs did little to warm one's heart. Nobody, neither soldiers, officials nor passengers smiled or seemed to have any inclination ever to do so, and there was no sign of any but the most dull and muted colours – and this was to be our home for the next two and a half years.

At last a friendly face – someone from the Embassy had arrived to meet us and to usher us through the Diplomatic Personnel Only gate at passport control thus avoiding a very long and slow moving queue. To our amazement we were then confronted by a barrage of friendly faces: someone had forgotten to tell us that all new Attachés were by tradition met at the airport by their colleagues in the Military Attaché Corps. They stood in a semicircle and we were introduced to each in turn – every country from Canada and Chad to Yugoslavia and Zambia, and I just knew I'd never remember all those names and faces. What was to be etched on my mind for all time though was how very smartly dressed all the wives were and how I wished I'd not thrown on comfortable 'travelling with two small children' type clothes complete with much loved, but decidedly grubby, toy puppy peeking out of one pocket. Before we were able to escape to the awaiting car there was one final surprise for us, or rather for Mike: apart from meeting fellow Attachés he was expected to make a speech! Master of the impromptu, this he did with no trouble. We arrived in Beijing in 1981, when there were few planes and few passengers, but this tradition of meeting and of saying goodbye to colleagues continued at least until 1990, when the airport was always busy. As the size of the Attaché Corps grew, so too did the amount of space they took up at the airport, to the extent at times of completely blocking the concourse – and I shall never forget the bemused expression on the face of a Chinese traveller who somehow managed to find himself and all his suitcases in the middle of the circle, standing next to the Attaché making his farewell and very emotional speech.

If the airport struck us as grey and colourless, then the streets seemed even more so. The road, lined with bare trees, passed through bare, dry farmland with the occasional glimpse of farm buildings and their occupants – all dressed in dull green overcoats and fur-lined hats with earflaps pulled tightly down. Progress was slow: the road was narrow and we always seemed to be stuck behind a tiny three-wheeler tractor and trailer or a mule cart, the largest of which were pulled by a horse, a mule and a donkey together. Any efforts on the Chinese driver's part to overtake was hampered by the fact that all traffic kept to the middle of the road to allow plenty of room for cyclists, the bicycle being the most common form of transport. As we neared the city the mule carts all turned off down side roads as they were only allowed into the city centre in the middle of the night – at all other times they had to circumnavigate Beijing on side roads. Farm houses were replaced by grey blocks of flats with small 'garden' areas outside – but no sign of any grass or plants, just grey dusty earth. Most flats seemed to have a balcony piled high with boxes, furniture, even bicycles. A few dim lights glowed in grey windows and huddled figures entered the few colourless shops – what a contrast this was to the constantly neon-lit streets of Hong Kong, but the conservation of energy here was guaranteed by the fact that the only light bulbs available were maximum 40 watts!

Foreigners living in Beijing were all housed ghetto-fashion in Diplomatic Compounds: blocks of flats arranged round a dust bowl of a garden and surrounded by a high wall, the two or three gates of which were guarded day and night by an armed soldier to check that only those Chinese with official passes entered. These young soldiers were always posted away from their home provinces and might come from an area thousands of miles distant: the climate, customs, and certainly foreigners, would be a constant source of amazement to them. The flat that was to be our home was in one of the older, Russian design blocks, flat number

51. It was, in fact, not the fifty first flat, but flat number one on the fifth floor. This rather unique numbering system – quite logical when you think about it – meant that flats weren't numbered 1,2,3,4 etc. but 11,12,13,14,21,22,23,24,31,32 etc. And then in some buildings the ground floor was called 'G' whilst in others it was called '1'...! Our building had an ancient lift operated by an unsmiling lady who switched it off when she went home in the evening, leaving us to use the dimly-lit stairs. We discovered that this was common practice and there was nearly a diplomatic incident when one high ranking foreigner suddenly left a banquet in the middle of his Chinese host's speech. Torn between anger at such rudeness and fear that he had offended in some way, the Chinese dignitary was eventually calmed by the explanation that the foreigner lived on the 16th floor and the lift was switched off at 7pm sharp!

Flat 51 was situated overlooking the garden/playpark at the back (the swing, see-saw etc. having been vandalised by the diplomatic children), and Beijing's main thoroughfare Chang An (Long Peace) at the front. Chang An was a very wide, grand street with almost as much road allocated to cyclists as to vehicles, the two being separated by low concrete and metal barriers. The road was lined with ornate, multi-globed lamps, but only a few of the bulbs were lit except on high days and holidays. Our accommodation was large and comfortable – except for the kitchen which for some reason had roughly the proportions of a bowling alley: so long and thin that it was impossible for two people to pass each other. Most welcome of all was the fact that the flat was beautifully warm – surprising considering there was no double glazing and the gaps round some of the window frames were clearly visible. The heating was all fed from one enormous central boiler and, lacking thermostats, the only way to regulate the temperature was to remove the heavy, ornate radiator covers and switch them on and off as required. As foreigners we were allowed constant heating, unlike the local Chinese population, who were only entitled to warmth for a few designated hours. When the sun shone (as it often did, low and bright in a wintry sky) many of the locals found it warmer to wrap up well and sit outside rather than stay indoors. We were in keeping with Chinese housing in one respect though: there was no hot water on tap and we relied on an electric heater over the kitchen sink and an amazing copper boiler in the bathroom, which really required the attentions of a Chief Stoker it had so many valves and knobs. It was certainly effective, as I discovered when I ran the first bath without realising that a metal tub would keep its heat for a long time – I had to wait forty minutes for it to cool down enough to get in.

After a few days in residence we began to be concerned about the condition of the electric wiring in the flat: every time we touched an electric appliance or fitting we received a shock. The Embassy 'Mr. Fixit' arrived and tested the system, but the only problem he found was that we averaged 169 volts rather than the usual 240. The static shocks, he explained, came in fact from a combination of the extreme cold, even more extreme dryness, and nylon in our carpets and clothes. He arranged for us to have a humidifier which would release at least two bucketsful of water into the atmosphere every day (the average humidity was below 15% compared with over 90% on the west coast of Scotland!) Over the weeks we picked up all manner of tips from other 'sufferers': never shake hands without first touching the wall to earth yourself, keep a cup of water by the bed (covered, to avoid drowning thirsty cockroaches) to drink the minute you awake or you'll be hoarse all day, use lashings of moisturising cream or you'll turn from plum to prune overnight and never wear anything except natural fibres unless you favour the clinging look. Despite all these precautions some amount of pain was inevitable – in those pre-remote control days someone still had to switch off the TV, and we had unwittingly brought with us a beautiful copper-topped coffee table which could give you a nasty shock if you even walked close to it, let alone touched it (to this day it is still called the 'shock table'). By far the worst 'offenders', however, were the light fittings, being made entirely of metal and only accessible by first climbing an all metal stepladder – we learnt also that the average life of a Chinese lightbulb is 5 weeks! This low humidity did have one or two good points though: washing dried almost as soon as it was hung up and no one was ever asked to dry dishes! The children also derived a great deal of pleasure out of rushing around on the carpets to build up a good 'charge' and then approaching us, hands outstretched and baby hair standing on end much like miniature creations of Dr. Frankenstein, intoning "Going to shock you".

The building itself was of largely wooden construction: beautiful to look at, but a great fire risk. The Embassy had fitted several smoke alarms which were tested frequently whenever our Sri Lankan neighbours burnt their dinner and the smoke crept under the front door. We discovered that you can't switch off a smoke alarm and the only way to silence one is to grab it off the wall and smother it under several thick duvets! Better safe than sorry certainly: one family from an unnamed African country ran in to financial difficulties when they were recalled home but their national budget could only run to one airfare. The husband was sent home, but wife and numerous children were left in Beijing, their money dwindling fast. When their electricity and gas were finally cut off, they begged food from friends and neighbours and cooked it over an open fire in the middle of the sitting room floor. The only other neighbours we ever came across during our occupancy of flat 51 were a large group of Cubans living directly above us – for 364 days of the year they were virtually unseen and unheard, but on one day, be it festival or birthday I don't know, they had the party to end all parties. It was the only time I ever saw a light fitting literally shaking and swinging from side to side as they danced overhead.

The more that China opened up relations with other countries, the greater the number of diplomats resident in Beijing, so it was not too many years after our arrival that 15 storey blocks of flats were mushrooming around the Embassy areas. Much more spacious than the older ones, these flats were still lacking a few little touches to make them like home, all of which could be achieved by the Embassy to which they were allocated, but changes were positively discouraged by the Diplomatic Services Bureau, the organisation responsible for our housing. Before any fitting of cupboards, shelving etc. was allowed you had to pay the DSB whatever they reckoned it would cost to take it all away again and restore the flat to 'its original state' upon your vacating the premises. The only major alteration we made to our flat was the replacement of the gas cooker – an ancient-looking metal contraption with two burners and an oven, none of which possessed any regulating controls: they were either 'on' or 'off', which made simmering and baking almost an impossibility. Lighting it was exciting too, although you did have a long-handled gas wand to allow you to distance yourself a little from the inevitable explosion. As well as housing becoming inadequate, so too did the number of Embassy buildings themselves, so a new diplomatic district was set up a few miles out of the city, some countries even being allowed to built their own Embassies in their national styles. Not only did that give some wonderful architectural sights but, as many of these newly arrived countries were Middle Eastern or Asian, their own small diplomatic shops stocked a wonderful range of spices.

The Embassy formed the centre of life for most British residents and tried to provide most of what was needed. It housed, apart from the offices themselves, a small library, stocked with some new books and a large number donated by people leaving for other posts. This was a much prized asset and used not just by ourselves but by the many English speaking countries with Embassies in China. Next to that was situated a tiny shop, packed floor to ceiling with all manner of imported goods. Because of the limited space, both for display and storage, and the comparatively slow turnover (it being open only to British Embassy personnel) the stock was equally limited and regulated by the likes and needs of the majority. If most people liked Cornflakes and Weetabix then that's what you'd be breakfasting on for the foreseeable future. It was actually less boring than it sounds and you certainly appreciated the choice afforded by shops in Hong Kong and UK when you got there. We soon learnt, too, that it paid to stockpile some items, as deliveries were infrequent. Before arriving in Beijing we had been given a list of items it was advisable to take in quantity from home; these included soap, toothpaste and shampoo: I assumed that Chinese people must surely keep clean, and decided to risk getting them locally. I was glad that I did: the cost of all items in the Embassy shop carried a transport and shop commission surcharge making them very expensive, and I found the many Chinese equivalents were often better. Some people refused to buy locally simply because the product was Chinese – one wife advised me to buy British toilet paper because "there are more sheets per roll", but at less than a quarter of the price for the local product, who's counting? Perhaps the least obvious, but certainly the most valuable, service provided for us was an Embassy nurse. Local medical care was little advanced from the 'bare-foot' stage at that time, and our own nurse took on the responsibilities of a G.P., but with no back-up on site. If anyone deserved a medal, she did.

The other great facilities provided by the Embassy were a small outdoor pool, tennis courts and a tiny bar 'The Bell', with all the atmosphere of a pub, and a large Amenities Hall suitable for indoor sports, plays etc. This hall also doubled as an earthquake shelter, the area under the stage being packed with emergency food supplies, bottled water, cooking stoves and the like. The threat of earthquake was a real one, and we all kept an emergency bag ready to hand in case of evacuation. Upon our arrival we were issued with a list of suggested items, which included dried food, soap, hat and gloves and - my favourite – clean underwear! I had visions of the British residents camping amongst the rubble, huddled round Primus stoves, but proud of the fact that at least their underwear was clean! Some official visitors from UK had been known to make disparaging remarks about misuse of taxpayers' money, but as the nearest public pool, sports or social facility was in Hong Kong, what the Embassy was able to provide was more appreciated than many people realised. One problem with the rather enclosed way of life was that you inclined to live solely with other Brits. and met few Chinese people. This was made all the more difficult by the suspicion of the locals who would stare unashamedly, and unsmilingly, at you and yet were afraid (a hang over from the Cultural Revolution maybe) to be seen talking to foreigners. They relaxed somewhat when they realised that we weren't Russians, and were naturally more at ease with our two blond babies to the extent that if I smiled I sometimes evoked a smile in response. Stories I had heard of Chinese people touching fair hair for luck must have originated in the south of China: no one here made any attempt to touch the children – we would be surrounded by a crowd of up to fifty locals, all staring and talking about us, but the minute we made to move on they parted like the Red Sea to let us through. I suppose we were more fortunate in our everyday dealings with local people than the Russians who lived in a completely self-contained, walled city of an Embassy with school, doctors, shops etc. and not a single Chinese employee.

After just a few days I realised that I didn't want to spend the next couple of years drinking coffee and complaining about 'them', my ayi, cook, tailor etc. There was only one answer – I had to learn Chinese. Mr. Lin, one of my Chinese teachers, was one of the tallest, thinnest men I'd ever seen. In fact the impression we have in the West of Chinese being small really only applies to those from the south: northerners are about the same average stature as ourselves. The first lessons consisted of pronunciation and tone drills – there being four tones, the mere change of sound changing the meaning of the word. I decided that there were enormous possibilities for confusion here, and was grateful for Mr. Lin's tip: always qualify your words if possible. For example, the word soup and sugar are the same (tang) except for the pronunciation, so to be totally sure you get what you want ask for meat or fish soup or white or red (our brown) sugar. The language is in many ways very logical and therefore easy to remember. A train (steam) is a 'fire vehicle', tap (running) water is 'water that comes by itself', a zip is a 'pull lock', yogurt is simply 'sour milk' and our assorted jackets, coats and sweaters are simply 'on top', 'big' and 'wool' clothes. Even the days of the week and months of the year are just numbered Day One, Day Two, Month One, Month Two etc. (with the exception of Sunday – 'Heaven Day') There aren't a myriad of tenses to worry about either. The only real problems I had with spoken Chinese were the way we looked at things as opposed to the Chinese way: if I asked for an opinion saying "I don't think that suits me, do you?" and Mrs. Yuan (our ayi or 'home help') answered in the affirmative, I assumed she meant it did suit me. In fact, she really meant "Yes, I agree with you, it doesn't suit you". 'Last week' translates as 'up week' and 'next week' as 'down week', which I always found very hard to remember as, being an optimist, I always thought of the future as 'up' rather than 'down'. When giving directions, the Chinese didn't refer to turning left or right, but of turning to the north or south etc. In the past this would have been used not just in directions, but in everyday life: a man visiting a dentist would refer to his teeth on the west being fine but those on the east being painful. The really difficult part of the language was the reading and writing of the characters, but we decided that my main need was to be able to communicate verbally, so I confined myself to recognition of the essential written words such as 'entrance', 'exit', 'no entry', 'ladies', 'gents' and 'toilet', plus the numerals. One of the greatest of Chairman Mao's achievements, to my mind, was the introduction of 'pinyin', a system of Romanising Chinese characters. This was to help eliminate the enormous illiteracy problem in China at that time, but it also helped foreigners enormously in their mastery of the spoken language. It did give rise to some moments of humour to the Western reader, as the pinyin words were often lumped together and written as one, thus playing cards were labelled 'puke' and leather shoes were advertised in a shop window as 'pixie'.

Chapter Two: Shopping

Once I felt I could manage a few words of Chinese I ventured forth to try my hand at shopping. The Friendship Store (there was one in every city frequented by foreigners) was for the sole use of foreigners, overseas Chinese, local employees of those two, and certain high ranking cadres. Along with so much of the Russian-influenced architecture in Beijing, the building was large and square with wide steps leading to doorways flanked by stone columns, and the rooms inside were vast and high-ceilinged. I first explored the ground floor where only food was sold – and what an eye-opener that was! There were a few very dry looking cakes and biscuits, and loaves of bread which came in black and heavy or white and heavy. Milk was sold in glass bottles with plastic caps and delicious natural yogurt in white ceramic pots with waxed paper covers. The words 'Beijing District Milk Factory - Yogurt' looked quite beautiful when written in ornate characters and I decided to collect these yogurt pots as vases, pencil holders etc. Eggs, rationed to locals but not to us, were sold by weight in brown paper bags which disintegrated if wet - never buy eggs on a rainy day! Cream, occasionally fresh, but often slightly sour could be found from time to time. It too was sold by weight - and you had to bring your own container. The rather limited delicatessen counter kept some strong-tasting sausages, ham which ranged from lean to stringy, and the most delicious pâté. The rather uninspiring fare was offset somewhat by the fact that it was all incredibly cheap and the assistants wore spotlessly white coats and were very careful not to touch money if they were to handle food. To pay, you put your notes and coins in a dish and the assistant handled them with tweezers. The second food hall specialised in greengrocery and meat – although specialised is perhaps the wrong word to describe the choices available. Potatoes were soft, sweet-tasting and a mass of eyes, and the only green vegetable was Chinese cabbage, but not the crisp ones we had been used to - these were limp and rubbery. There were a few tomatoes, their red colour barely visible amongst the black blotches that covered their skins and ran through their flesh, and some bruised apples. One of the problems in China at that time was transportation: perishable produce from the fertile southern regions could not be sent north fast enough to keep it in saleable condition. Ironically, around the upper walls of the food hall were brightly coloured murals depicting scenes from the countryside with smiling, rosy-cheeked peasant girls harvesting an abundance of perfect fruit and vegetables.

In the meat department there was a large marble slab on which were chunks of very fatty pork of unrecognisable cuts - and a cow. The cow was dead, partially skinned and headless, but unmistakeably a cow. Assuming it was about to be expertly 'butchered' into various cuts of beef, I waited around before buying any, but watching other shoppers I soon realised my mistake. You simply asked for however many 'jin' (pounds) of beef you wanted and a suitable sized lump was cut off from one end - and none dared incur the wrath of the assistant by asking for a particular piece of meat: you took what you were given! If you had time to spare, you could try to estimate how many more beef shoppers were needed to reach a part of the cow you wanted, and then return to the counter later! Minced beef was simply another lump cut off the carcass and thrown into a mincer together with a lump of fat from under the counter. I found, in one corner, a small freezer with packages of meat in, but they were so frosted up that you couldn't see what you were buying. There was also a blackboard with lists of fish – including tuna and salmon – and poultry such as 'hen'. 'young hen' and 'cock', but no indication as to what was actually available: you just pointed to each item on the board in turn until one was produced. The fish came complete with head, entrails and scales, but at least the chickens, thin little things, were plucked!

The quality of food generally was poor - apart from the very solid bread and the sawdust biscuits, the flour had weevils in it so as you rolled out pastry you had to pick them out with a pin. (If you transferred the flour to a glass jar you had, within days, a wonderful wildlife observatory with their intricate system of tunnels). The beef was only suitable for mincing or stir-frying in very thin slices: after 18 hours in a slow cooker it was still too tough even to cut and when I finally resorted to mincing it up I achieved beefburgers with the consistency of soft shoe leather. Supplies were erratic and unknown - so shopping was a fulltime occupation.

Bread, fruit, milk and vegetables were all delivered at a different time of the day and no one seemed to know what time that would be, and unless you happened to be there soon after a delivery they sold out anyway. I soon developed a whole new outlook to meal planning - no longer did I make a list of what shopping I needed, I simply bought what was available and decided afterwards how to make a meal out of it. The assistants didn't help either, not caring about the customer one bit. This came from the 'iron rice bowl' system (you all ate from the communal bowl no matter how much work you'd put in) whereby there was no advantage in working any better or harder than anyone else as you'd still be paid just the same. It was not unusual to wait some minutes to be served while they drank their tea, chatted etc. and on one occasion I watched fascinated as an older assistant taught a younger one how to blow her nose - onto the floor of the vegetable department. Chinese people thought it most insanitary to blow one's nose into a handkerchief and then carry it around in your pocket all day - much better to hold one nostril shut and blow the other with great force onto the road, pavement or concrete floor where it would be cleaned away (by someone else!). On another occasion I heard a customer, seeing a very long queue at the delicatessen counter, ask the assistant if butter was sold there. Being assured it was, he joined the queue. When it was finally his turn to be served he asked for a pack, only to be told that there wasn't any. He had made the mistake of asking if it was sold there, not if there was any, and was given the literally correct answer! We gradually got to recognise the least and most helpful of the assistants and gave them nicknames such as 'stroppy of bread' and 'pigtails of milk'. Shopping taught me perhaps the most used Chinese word - "meiyou". It literally means 'no have', but in general usage can be taken to be "we've run out", "we don't stock that", "it's off" and even "I can't understand what you want and don't intend to waste my time thinking about it anyway".

The second and third floors of the Friendship Store were a complete contrast - cottons and exotic silks almost given away, Western and Chinese dinner services, a few clothes, shoes and toiletries, and the odd toy or child's bike. Cotton in any form was rationed for Chinese people, but foreigners were allowed as many cotton coupons as they wanted. No matter what you were buying you had to inspect it very carefully - top quality goods were for export and only 'seconds' reached the local market. Also, quality control was unknown. Shoe buckles and zips had a lifespan of days and you were expected to try to pull a bike to pieces to test it before purchase. One reason for this poor quality was that articles were not always made by specialist factories. If a steel works or machinery plant was short of orders they would keep the workforce employed by producing alternative goods: pushchairs made by a tank factory were commonplace, as were sweaters machine-knitted by welders. If there was no quality control, there was no copyright either, and one of the most prominent creams for sale in the cosmetics department was 'Oil of Ulan" in its unmistakeable copy packaging. Toys were of particularly poor quality, many being made of tin and having razor sharp edges, but amongst them could be found the most exquisite kites made from fine silk and thin strips of bamboo, and painted to depict flowers, butterflies or literary and mythical heroes and heroines. Some were modelled in the shape of birds, or dragons whose bodies were made up of ten or more sections, giving a kite metres long. Unlike all the other goods on sale, these kites were well made and flew to perfection. Clothing was very cheap, even if not made to last, but you had to take care of the sizing (there being nowhere to try them on). Chinese women are narrower of hip and smaller of bottom than their Western counterparts, so it was imperative to use a tape measure, and your own one at that as a Chinese inch equalled one and a half of ours. Similarly the beautifully appliquéd and embroidered bedlinen proved to be too narrow for Western beds and pillows.

Aladdin's cave would have paled into insignificance beside the displays of embroideries, cloisonné, lacquerware, jade, gold, camphorwood, plants crafted from semiprecious stones and delicate silk flowers. How could such breathtakingly beautiful things come from such a grey, depressed-looking country?

When, after a few more lessons and a lot of homework, I felt more confident in my linguistic efforts, I explored the local shops, few as there were. The window displays looked dull and colourless by day or night and inside, the shelves were almost bare, the few items there were being spread around to make it appear better stocked. The largest shop in the vicinity of the foreigners' housing sold household goods: a few basic and not too sturdy looking wooden chairs and tables and a couple of children's tricycles. Also a thin metal stand designed to hold an enamel washbowl decorated with flowers, and a place to put soap and hang a towel. This was an essential space-saver in the locals' tiny, crowded rooms with no running water. The other popular household items for sale were large metal thermos flasks, much larger than any I'd seen before and so effective that they kept water really hot for up to twelve hours. Below the cracked glass counter were tubes of toothpaste, very hard toothbrushes and what appeared to be very good quality towels. The rest of the vast shop space seemed to be quickly filled with curious onlookers staring at, and talking about, me! In all shops, including the Friendship Store, all mathematical calculations were done on an abacus at incredible speed – faster, I expect, than we could operate a calculator. The currency system itself was rather hard to grasp as there were two distinct types of paper money: 'Renminbi' (RMB) or People's Money and 'Foreign Exchange Certificate' (FEC). FEC was only to be used by foreigners and some high ranking cadres (who could use RMB too). We were not really meant to ever handle RMB and it was never accepted in the Friendship Store. This did unfortunately give rise to a black market – if a Chinese person had access to the Store (e.g. as an Embassy employee) and FEC, he could purchase items never available to the man in the street. (Apropos of nothing; the Chinese word for 'man in the street' is far more poetic 'old hundred names').

After the depressed local shops it was a joy to discover Wangfujing, near the centre of the city, and the main shopping thoroughfare. Near to the street itself we came across a large meat, fruit and vegetable market: if we thought the quality we'd seen in the Friendship Store was bad, we then realised just what the local population had to put up with. At one stall the seller was cutting the many mouldy parts out of apples and returning them to the counter where people queued eagerly to buy them, or what was left of them. The mainstay for vegetables was the Chinese cabbage (*baicai*), a wonderfully versatile foodstuff. This was sold not in shops but in the street, where enormous piles, almost walls, of them would be seen once a year. You would buy an entire year's supply and stack them outside on your balcony or small area of ground, covering them with a thick cotton quilt. Every week the cabbages had to be inspected and turned and any dead leaves removed. We kept our own pile of them on a balcony and I was amazed to find that although many of the outer leaves had had to be discarded, much of the cabbage was still suitable for cooking and the 'hearts' were still edible raw after many months. The meat in the market looked none too fresh, but as it was so terribly cold it kept reasonably well. In the hot summer months a Chinese family (very few had fridges) would have to shop before each meal – there being three cooked meals a day!

Another shop that had quite a queue outside wasn't in fact selling anything, but accepting things for sale: anything which could be reused or recycled including orange peel which was made in to medicine. This was an economy, I came to realise, where nothing was wasted. Apart from the usual recycling of paper and glass there was a shop where felt-tipped pens could be refilled (you had to do the messy job yourself!) and another which repaired the very inexpensive inflatable plastic toys. These toys were very popular with Chinese families whose living conditions were very cramped, as they could be deflated and stored in the minimal amount of space. I saw a young girl going to collect her milk ration (only available to young children, pregnant women and nursing mothers) carrying a specially designed, home-made basket. It was exactly the size to hold two milk bottles and had been beautifully woven in two colours using the plastic strips used to band packing crates. Chinese tea mugs (those with lids on) seemed very cheap to us, but obviously not to the locals. They coveted screw-top jamjars (not easy to find here), so convenient to keep your tealeaves in and carry to work, then add water and drink. To jazz them up a bit, and to act as an insulator, you could buy on almost any street corner a stretchy cover hand-woven from thin strips of plastic. They were produced at incredible speed and the designs often incorporated a panda and the characters for Beijing.

The need to reuse and recycle also led to great ingenuity: a sign for a bicycle repair shop was made from an old wheel rim with the character 'mend' in the middle fashioned from various bits and pieces of old bikes. It cost nothing, but got the message across with great clarity. Nor was recycling confined to small, everyday articles: in many a children's playpark around the city an old Air Force jet - minus engine, was parked for children to play in! During our time in Beijing we also found the need to conserve our limited resources – especially lemons! Those were the days when gin and tonic was *the* drink and lemons were almost unobtainable, so it was great one-upmanship to produce a slice, no matter how small, or how old. On the very rare occasion that they were to be found we would buy as many lemons as we could, slice them thinly and freeze them. After each cocktail or dinner party the slices would be rinsed, and refrozen for use the next time! As a further effort at conservation we would keep the two ends of each fruit for our own use – but still use them over and over again. There was a great market in secondhand foreign goods, for which the Friendship Store Purchasing Department kept a list of prices to be paid. My electric sewing machine was irreparably damaged in transit to China but I thought I might get something for it as a source of spare parts. The 'buyer' however insisted that he would pay the full price quoted in his list – this seemed ridiculous to me until I later realised that the machine would undoubtedly be used as a prototype by a Chinese factory. This system was commonplace – buy just one and copy it – much to the fury of foreign companies trying to break in to the Chinese market. The man at the Purchasing Department was at great pains to point out that, having been given a price, I must sell there and then; should I return later the price would drop by 75%. Apparently many foreign residents had been using the Department as a source of valuation before attempting to sell the goods elsewhere.

The department store of Beijing was called One Hundred Products Big Building (*Bai Huo Da Lou*). It certainly had more than 100 products, but still not much choice or stock. I tried to find a water sprayer for Mrs. Yuan to use while ironing (the previous one had broken after a few weeks – as did so many things here), but it was 'meiyou' so she just had to continue in her old fashioned method of taking a mouthful of water and spitting a fine spray between her teeth. Everyday items were more readily available than I had found elsewhere: tea mugs with lids, crockery, string (which broke under any pressure), toiletries and a wide selection of electric plugs. This latter was necessary as in our flat alone we had a mixture of sockets ranging from flat to round, 2 to 3 pin, large to small. Also a plug bought in Shanghai did not necessarily fit a socket in Beijing. Inspired by the cheap cotton material (an export reject judging from its pattern 'ABCPEFJ') I bought some for Anna and then went to another department in search of a zip. Any idea of a specific colour or even length was soon abandoned: I got the feeling that I should be grateful to find one at all, no matter the colour or the fact that it was 6 inches too long. The adults' clothing had little to offer in the way of fashion or colour, ('Mao' suits still being very common) but were perfectly suited to the winter weather: thick woollen underwear, corduroy shoes thickly padded with natural cotton and wonderful overcoats called '*dayis*'. Occasionally seen in deep blue, these dayis were almost invariably made of dull green cotton. Between the outer coat and its lining were several inches of cotton wadding, making the coat very heavy to wear but impervious to the coldest Siberian wind. They also served as makeshift duvets when travelling or even as pillows (lay your dayi flat and fold the sleeves across the chest; then fold the coat into three, and you have a pillow). I had wondered for some time why there seemed to be so many surgeons walking the streets still wearing their white face masks – now all was revealed. The masks were for everyone's use, and made of thick cotton. Ever resourceful, the Chinese had overcome the problem of breathing in freezing air, the annoyance of a scarf slipping off from around the face and the discomfort of wet condensation on wool. The white masks were thick enough to warm the air breathed in, were firmly attached by tapes around the ears and absorbed moisture. All these clothes would have been wonderful in a Scottish winter, except that they were not waterproof – unnecessary here as it never rained in winter.

In stark contrast to the greys, greens and deep blues of the adults' clothes, the children's section was a mass of colour, but still not for the fashion-conscious. Of one basic, practical design, the jackets and trousers were both equally thickly padded, but the trousers for toddlers were all open at the crotch. Chairman Mao had declared that nappies were 'bourgeois' and not to be used and so small children were soon taught to crouch down whenever necessary, thereby doing away with the traumas of 'potty training', nappy rash etc. You would often see a small child squatting by the side of the road, but they never seemed to feel the cold. In the far north where the temperatures were much lower, children also wore a thick padded cotton 'apron' to stop the wind blowing onto their bare bottoms. The clothes were not only colourful, but made of an amazing variety of materials: green and blue spots, pink and red stripes, multi-coloured abstracts – obviously a case of using whatever material was available and not worrying at all about the fact that outer fabric clashed violently with lining and they in turn clashed with the trousers. Once you had literally fought your way through the scrum of shoppers at the counter you didn't ever ask for a particular design you'd spotted on the shelf (it wouldn't be available in more than a couple of sizes), but simply sat your child on the counter and asked for clothes, shoes etc. to fit. A few sizes too large didn't matter either, you were thankful to find anything, and many an adult could be seen with rolled up trousers and turned back cuffs. The only winter item I didn't find were woollen hats and scarves but the source of these was discovered at the bus stops – mothers and grannies standing, or crouching, waiting with needles clicking at amazing speed, and other travellers keeping a careful distance as the needles were pointed at both ends and very sharp.

Weighed down with shopping, I bought a couple of nylon/string bags – there being no polythene carriers here – and explored a few more of the shops Wangfujing had to offer. There were several 'speciality' shops including one selling fur hats and leather gloves, one selling all manner of musical instruments, some of which I'd never seen before, and another selling 'chops' or seals. These were made of stone, the top usually carved with a flower or dragon design and the bottom carved with the characters or name of your choice. You could use our alphabet or have your name translated phonetically into Chinese characters (which worked well on some names, but less well on others: one friend's surname put into characters meant 'pull a dead horse'). Should you actually plan to use your chop as a stamp (as could be seen on all old calligraphy scrolls and paintings), it was necessary to buy a shallow china bowl with a lid, containing bright red paste in which to dip the chop. This paste was only available in red, except if you were the Emperor, in which case you used vermilion. The Emperor possessed numerous chops and no edict was recognised unless stamped with one of them – it being easy to forge a signature, but not to carve the intricate design of the seals – and they were kept carefully guarded lest some over-ambitious official decided to issue orders of his own using the Emperor's name. The number he was allowed was in fact limited in the 1700s so as to keep a better check on their whereabouts: no Emperor would possess more than 25. (That number was rumoured to have been chosen because it was the sum of the odd numbers 1,3,5,7 and 9 and therefore symbolised the supremacy of Imperial authority and the unity and prosperity of the Empire.)

Further along Wangfujing I also discovered a shop specialising in tea, a beverage consumed in China for around 4,000 years and having more varieties produced here than in any other country. I bought small packages of black, green, Wulong and scented to try, and was given instructions as to the best way to prepare it. A small amount of leaves should be put in a pot or a mug with a lid, and boiling water added. After a few minutes' brewing time the water should be drained off, as the tea would be bitter at this stage, and replaced with fresh boiling water. Once the tea had been drunk, the leaves should not be discarded as with Indian tea, but used several times more, the taste getting sweeter. On no account should anything such as milk or sugar be added unless you were a Tibetan, when you might favour a knob of butter and a pinch of salt, or a Mongolian who would prefer to add salt and a dash of mare's milk.

The sheer number of people entering and leaving local shops meant that the doors were forever swinging and letting awful draughts in, so in winter the doors were replaced by incredibly heavy padded leather curtains, which you literally had to force yourself between – very effective they were too.

A treasure hunt would be the best way to describe shopping in Beijing at that time. Toilet brushes took weeks to find, and then only in one shop literally miles the other side of the city. Broom heads could also be purchased there, but handles – well, they were a 20 minute cycle ride to the south. Christmas cards could be spotted in June (export surplus, as no one celebrated it in China), but envelopes that would vaguely match in size would mean a trip to the stationery store – which also sold toilet paper (quite logical when you think about it). Then there were the completely unexpected finds: children's sandals with squeakers in the soles (limited life, thankfully), magnetic acupressure insoles made by the March 8th Shoe Factory and The Central Iron and Steel Research Institute. The least hideously ornate kitchen clock we could find turned out to play a different tune every hour of a 12 hour cycle: what it didn't do was then chime the hour itself. Thinking to have been incredibly clever, I learnt the corresponding tune and time, only to find that when the battery was replaced the two no longer corresponded anyway. Funnily enough, only one of the tunes was Chinese, the rest including such gems as 'Home Sweet Home', 'Happy Birthday' and 'Clementine'. (This was probably the only mechanical item we bought in China which worked for more than a few months). The important thing we learnt about shopping was that you never knew when you'd suddenly come across something irresistible, and it was guaranteed to be a 'one off' – if you didn't buy it there and then, you'd as likely as not never see it again.

One shop frequented almost entirely by the foreign population was the so-called 'Theatre Shop', which specialised in old theatrical costumes and antique jewellery and ornaments. Amongst the many unusual items to be found were silver filigree nail protectors – the elite of the past had no need to do manual work so grew their nails very long and these protectors, apart from their obvious purpose, also brought attention to their hands and therefore their status in society. What appeared to be a flat wooden spoon opened out to reveal portable scales used to weight herbal medicines, and tiny wooden carvings that once adorned temples were piled on a table, along with walnuts intricately carved with scenes from Buddhist scripture. On a shelf were displayed tiny glass snuff bottles decorated with 'typical' Chinese landscapes, but these were painted onto the *inside* of the bottles, using a very fine paintbrush with bristles mounted at right angles to the handle. Unable to resist any of these treasures I also bought a Chinese Opera headdress, so ornate, but for hanging on the wall only – their heads must have been tiny compared with ours. By far the most unusual 'find' were household shrines from the days when religion was allowed in China. These 'God boxes', as the foreigners affectionately called them, were about 2 feet high and carved and painted to represent miniature temples, but during our stay in the country the last were sold and none ever appeared again. We were fortunate to purchase two, one of which had 4 characters carved on it, the first two being the same as those used to make the name 'Farr'. Mrs. Yuan told us that many beautiful items once owned by many Chinese families, had been destroyed or thrown away in terror during the Cultural Revolution, as they were considered bourgeois. As more and more diplomats and businessmen took up residence, so the market for things both old and Chinese blossomed, but 'buyer beware' – no item deemed to be an antique was allowed out of the country unless certified by the Antiquities Department and marked with one of their red wax seals. To avoid long delays in shipment and a great deal of hassle, it was always advisable to have all your purchases examined before packing to leave China at the end of your tour, this examination being carried out by a dear old man who looked older than most of the antiques he was so avidly guarding.

If you could make up a small group it was sometimes possible to visit a handicrafts factory, where you would see all those things that were for export only and which you couldn't find in the shops and where, in the factory's own shop, you might just be lucky enough to find a fraction of those things actually for sale. In some of the factory shops you might even find articles not even made there, but either put on display to fill up the shelves or as a reciprocal arrangement with another establishment. Upon your arrival at any factory you were first ushered into an anteroom, seated in chairs arranged around the edge of the room and given a cup of Chinese tea. The manager then told you all about the factory, the number of workers and the annual output and income – omitting to mention the actual take home pay of the workers. A description of the products themselves was followed, unfailingly, by a request for your comments and suggestions as to any improvements that could be made. Rather a rhetorical question and best always diplomatically countered with polite praise of their obvious success. These factory tours were an eye-opener, both in your understanding and appreciation of the product and in the appalling working conditions. The humble carpet has far more of a history than I imagined: early nomadic tribes wove basic rugs from the wool of their sheep, which skill developed until by about 200BC the carpets were of such a high standard that they were often presented as tribute gifts to the Emperor and his court. In order to curry favour with a superior you would have woven for him a carpet with a unique design unlike any other – but only the Emperor himself would allow a yellow one bearing a dragon. So valuable did they become that during the time of the Opium War carpets became tradeable items. Walking around the factory I saw designs that we never see – 'ethnic' minority art, scenes from remote areas of China etc. There were many of the traditional designs of course, and quite a few of the sculpted flower patterns, which I'd always imagined were produced using different lengths of wool. In fact the length was uniform, but areas were cut shorter once the carpet was finished, using electric shears. Unlike carpets, I'd never liked cloisonné very much, but came to appreciate it far more having seen the painstaking process of glueing thin copper wires onto a vase and endlessly filling the tiny spaces with enamel, then firing, filling, firing again many, many times. In one factory I discovered embroidered pictures worked onto fine, almost transparent, white silk, the pictures being reversible: on one side of the material would be a ginger coloured embroidered kitten and on the reverse the same kitten would be worked in grey silk thread, and no sign of the ginger silk showing through. Be it carpets, cloisonné, lacquerware or jade-carving, the one common denominator seemed to be a 40 watt light bulb and a complete disregard for safety. How such beautiful and intricate work was produced in the gloom of a single bulb amazed me – even finest embroidery was allowed no better lighting, and I suspect that the eyesight must have suffered terribly. Pieces of jade and semi-precious stones were cut prior to carving on a lethal looking electric cutter with no protection for the hands, which were not even graced with a pair of gloves. With so many people available to fill these factory places the occasional accident proved to be no inconvenience to the management whatsoever – an injured worker could easily be replaced. Callous behaviour was not the reason for this, more a blind practicality and total lack of education as regards 'health and safety'. (When Mike later visited a shipyard, he was delighted to see that the message was beginning to get home: a 'supervisor' was wearing hard hat, safety boots, goggles etc. – but he turned out to be a visiting foreigner). Looking round the workshops of the factories dealing with jade and precious stones, I was surprised to see such valuable raw materials simply piled in a corner awaiting cutting, carving or polishing. Such was the unsophisticated, genuine honesty of these workers, that it did not occur to them to steal. If we, in the West, ever manage to educate them in modern working techniques and conditions, do we also run the risk or introducing our lower moral codes?

Chairman Mao once decided that sparrows were destroying too many of the country's crops and decreed that they were to be eliminated. To this end the entire population waged war on the poor birds and those not actually killed were frightened away by the banging and crashing of saucepans, metal bowls etc. until they died of exhaustion, being unable to land and rest. (It was later realised that with no sparrows to eat the insects a whole new problem emerged). Sparrows slowly returned over the years, but the vast majority of birds found in the city were kept in cages as pets, the keeping of anything else, except for fish, being illegal for city-dwellers. (During the Cultural Revolution some people were so frightened of being thought in any way Western that they even threw their goldfish into the rivers). Should you live in the countryside you were allowed to keep dogs, which in fact was a very sensible law considering the cramped living conditions and total absence of suitable dog-walking areas in the cities. Pet birds were predominantly the hobby of elderly, retired men, and whole markets were devoted to the sale of birds, cages, feed and all manner of other accoutrements. The cages were beautifully fashioned, mostly in bamboo, and ranged from utilitarian to three-storey exotic, and contained not plastic but china food and water bowls, painted with flowers or dragons. Even the miniature watering cans and chutes used to top up water and food were fashioned in brass and copper. I had never been too happy seeing birds in cages, but I came to think that the Chinese ones had lives equally fulfilled and certainly a good deal safer than their wild counterparts. In fine weather their cages were hung outside in the air where they would sing for hours. To ensure they, and their owners, kept fit they would be taken for a 'walk' every day, weather permitting. A thick, blue cotton made-to-measure cover would be put over the cage and zipped up and then it would be carried to the nearest park. Whilst in transit the cage would be swung quite violently back and forth as the owner strode along – it seemed very cruel to the bird inside, but my visions of a seasick occupant were totally wrong. In the gloom of the covered cage there was no disorientation and the regular swinging motion mimicked the action of branches swaying in the wind – the bird naturally used wings, leg muscles etc. to keep his balance and got plenty of healthy exercise. Upon arrival at the park, the cover was removed and the cage hung in a tree in close proximity to other cages: as the men sat and talked, discussed their birds, played chess etc. the birds 'talked' avidly to their temporary neighbours. During our time in Beijing many of the bird markets were 'discovered' by foreign residents and later by tourists, which gradually led to a change in them: terrapins, water snakes, white mice, chipmunks began to appear for sale, sadly kept in totally unsuitable conditions leading to not a few deaths.

Another great hobby for the retired local population was 'flowerpot gardening': with no gardens the city dwellers became experts in house plant care and cultivation, growing the most beautiful and exotic blooms.

Some shrub type plants with woody stems were often patiently trained over many years so that the stems grew in intricate lattice patterns: and then there were the much-prized bonsais. We never seemed to have the same success with any plants we tried to grow, possibly because our flats were too hot in winter and too air-conditioned in summer. Packets of seeds were unheard of (although a few imported ones did appear in the last few months of our time in China) and so, hoping to brighten up our balconies, I brought some back from a trip to the U.K. Potting compost was far too heavy to transport as well, so I went to our local plant shop and asked for a small sack of earth in which to plant my precious seeds. The assistant rummaged around and produced four large pots with very dead plants in them. These she removed and tossed into a corner, tipped the dry, totally nutrient-bereft earth into a bag and demanded the equivalent of one pound – which I was too amazed not to pay. Needless to say the seeds never amounted to much, but we found the answer to brighten up the flat – artificial flowers. Not, I hasten to add, the gaudy plastic ones, but exquisite silk creations that were impossible to tell apart from the real thing unless you touched them. It was possible to find them occasionally in Wangfujing, but a friend put us on to the specialist silk flower shop to the south of the city, the Funeral Flower Shop – for that was their use, to make wreathes to put on graves. Entering the shop it was impossible to think of such sombre occasions as funerals, for it was like stepping into the centre of a rainbow – every colour and shade imaginable. Searching round the shelves we also discovered ornate paper streamers and decorations of the sort that used to be seen at Christmas time years ago. The one disadvantage of silk as opposed to plastic was the problem of cleaning, but immersed in a polythene bag with a little salt and given a good shake, they came out as clean as new. A Chinese friend saw me doing this and a few days after proudly presented me with some plastic roses. "Look, all you have to do with these modern flowers is to wash them under the tap. Now isn't that so much better." I suppose it's all a matter of taste!

Another area where Chinese tastes changed to become modern to their way of thinking, and sadly spoilt to mine, was regarding furniture.

Old wooden chests; sturdy, carved, adorned with wonderful brass fittings and a unique padlocking system I'd seen nowhere else: wardrobes of incredible height to accommodate long robes: chairs that were so comfortable they needed no cushions: document boxes: jewellery boxes – the list was endless, and all made to last of thick, seasoned wood. But they were heavy and took up a lot of room – fine in the old, grand houses, but less so in a small flat, so the popular replacement was lightweight chipwood covered with formica and with a probable lifespan of just a few years. They didn't even seem to be very well made in the first place with drawers that stuck and doors that warped and mirrors that would have been a great hit in a funfair, but they were smaller, lighter and above all MODERN. The only good thing that I saw coming out of this was that all the beautiful old furniture was sold off cheaply to the foreigners – cheaply, that was, until the sellers realised they had a ready market and the price rocketed.

There being so many beautiful things to be found at ridiculously low prices it was naturally very tempting to send some of them home to friends and family - the choosing of the gifts was easy, the dispatching of them quite another matter. There were a reasonable number of post offices dotted around the city, although letter writing was still a more infrequent occupation than in the U.K., but only one was able to deal with foreign-bound letters and parcels. It was situated in a side street in 'downtown' Beijing and, as everywhere else, queuing was unheard of. Having fought your way to a place at the counter you had to show the contents of your parcel to the clerk and only when he, or she, was satisfied could you wrap the gift – only there was nowhere to wrap it. Were you lucky enough to pick a time when the post office was less crowded than usual, you might find an empty corner where you could squat down and even find a bit of floor space to lay out paper, sellotape, scissors etc. but usually your only hope was to balance on one leg like a stork and use the other, raised, knee as a table. With the increased number of foreign residents over the years a new International Post Office was built near to one of the Diplomatic Housing compounds. It was an amazing contrast – people queued, there were tables with pairs of scissors tied to them, pots of messy glue to stick envelopes and stamps, counters selling brown paper and large envelopes, a desk where you could arrange a subscription to your favourite (Chinese) magazine, even a place to buy sweets and, above all, lots and lots of room. For sending parcels within China the traditional wrapping wasn't paper: your item was placed in a pillowcase-sized cotton bag with plaited drawstring, and the address written onto the bag itself. (Durable, beatheable and washable, I still use these bags to pack and separate clothes before putting into a suitcase).

When we returned to China after a mere three years the changes were enormous. Free markets had sprung up on almost every street corner, selling a much greater variety of fruit and vegetables than we'd ever seen before. The transportation system had improved so much that produce such as bananas, peaches and pineapples were arriving regularly from the south throughout the summer months and new government legislation allowed farmers to sell privately anything produced in excess of their commune's annual quota. (The down side was that if they had a bad year and fell below quota they had to make up the difference in cash.) The wonderful array of food was matched by the multitude of colours seen on the shoppers themselves. Gone were the drab greys and blues and the 'Mao suits', except on a few of the older traditionalists. Brightly coloured Western styles were worn by the younger generation, and even skirts could be seen in the summer – the effect rather spoilt by the wearing of knee-length nylon socks with short skirts. Makeup could also be seen worn openly: a great shame, as Chinese girls had a natural beauty and wonderful skin that needed no enhancing, and the effect could border on the grotesque. Young people of the opposite sex now dared to hold hands in public places. What a contrast to the time when just the merest glimpse of a bright blouse might accidently be seen under a grey jacket: even Mrs. Yuan became bold enough to wear a skirt indoors in the height of summer, although she was still enough of a conformist to the old ways that she would rush away and change back into trousers the minute Mike arrived home. Her husband spent days searching for a blue shirt in his large size (he'd worn white ones all his life) because he wanted to show his workmates that in the new, modern, more affluent society he could afford more than one. (And to think that years back affluence was judged more on the number of concubines you possessed, not the number of shirts!) The majority of these bright, new fashions were sold in street markets and were either rejected or excess to requirements export orders, so although you could pick up amazing bargains you had to check seams, zips etc. carefully in case they were the cause of the cancellation.

In both food and clothing markets there were four different prices: foreigners, Chinese, Renminbi and Foreign Exchange Certificates, and bargaining was essential. FEC had by that time become in such demand by a certain section of the Chinese youth that you were constantly being hassled by young men, and even some women, whispering "change-a-money". Every now and again this black market would get out of hand and tourists would start to complain about being accosted every time they stepped foot outside their hotels, so the government would order an immediate clampdown and increased police presence on the streets. They would also announce the imminent abolition of FEC, causing the illegal hoarders and dealers to get shot of it as quickly as possible, for how were they to know that the threat would not be carried out, as it wasn't – twice!

Bird markets also expanded dramatically over the years and many branched out into toy stalls and 'antiques' aimed at the tourists. At the largest and busiest one you could even have a haircut: the itinerant street barbers coming from an old and long tradition. Confucian teaching ruled that your hair was given to you by your parents and was therefore all but sacred and not to be misused: it could be washed and combed but never cut. Imagine the reaction when the Manchus overran the country and decreed that all men must shave the fronts of their heads (and plait the back into the well-known 'queue'). Anyone failing to comply would be forcibly taken to the Manchu soldiers, who set up the first 'barber stations' around the city. Resistance would lead to an even closer shave – execution! The need for barbers (or head shavers) had been created and some of the Han Chinese, who were allowed to apply for business licences, set themselves up as barbers, either itinerant or in static sheds. As time went on they branched out into other fields, including massage and bone-setting – fortunately the latter was in time taken over by the medical profession, but their expertise at haircutting and massage went from strength to strength.

Government-owned shops had undergone some drastic changes too: the Friendship Store had already exchanged the dead cow for lumps of frozen meat – indistinguishable because of the thick, frosted polythene wrapping: the thickness of the packing was much appreciated as it was rumoured that the freezers were switched off overnight to save electricity. Polythene and plastic seemed to have taken over everywhere: biscuits, bread, eggs all came packaged, and the beautiful ceramic yogurt pots were virtually nonexistent. Milk bottles had been replaced by floppy plastic packets and it was even possible to have it delivered to your flat, although there was little finesse in the service as they threw them from the lift in the vague direction of your door. Surprisingly few of them split open! This rather lackadaisical attitude which we had nearly always encountered before had all but disappeared from the assistants at the Friendship Store, who not only spoke very passable English but wore smart uniforms and seemed keen to serve you - the 'iron rice bowl' had perhaps gone forever. Nor was it only the foreigners who were treated to such modernisation – supermarkets were opening up everywhere, creating cheaper shopping and employment: the first one to open in the city employed 53 people to process and package the food, 8 accountants, 8 assistants and 8 guards against shoplifting.

When we had first arrived in China and had to exist on local produce and the stocks kept by the Embassy shop, the chance of a trip to Hong Kong with its wonderful foodstuffs was like Christmas, but by the late 80s Hong Kong had virtually come to us. Western-style joint venture hotels had popped up like mushrooms and at least three of them had their own food shops. By far the largest and best stocked (by Dairy Farm, Hong Kong) was to be found in the Holiday Inn Lido Hotel, which boasted not just a delicatessen and bakery, but a full supermarket selling just about everything from American breakfast cereals to cat food – at a very high price. I seldom used it because of the price, especially when expected to pay more than double for local produce! Hotel shops were open to all foreigners, but for diplomats only the Chinese started a Diplomatic Shop, selling some food and alcohol, TVs, stereos and other electrical goods. Again I found this of limited use and I was totally put off when, having queued for ages to purchase blank video tapes, I was told that I would have to have my receipt cleared by the Customs Office who had just shut for an hour's lunch break.

Undoubtedly the improvements to the quality of shopping for both foreigners and locals was for the good but it did in many cases lead the younger Chinese to genuinely believe that everything in the West was so much better. No matter what the cost they would always try to buy an imported alternative: very wise in the case of the Smarties lookalikes which tasted awful, but a total waste of money when delicious Hainan coffee was spurned in favour of an inferior, imported alternative. Susceptibility to Western advertising was high too, and whereas we had become sceptical over years of exposure, the Chinese were inclined to believe all the manufacturers' claims.

With the exception of a few luxuries such as marmalade, baked beans and Weetabix I preferred to shop locally, for the Chinese diet seemed very healthy – and a whole lot cheaper. There was one occasion, however, when we were very grateful for the presence of the Lido and the Diplomatic Shop. All our wines and spirits were ordered duty free once or twice a year from the U.K., and were sent overland in the summer and by air in winter, as land 'shipments' had to pass through areas with sub-zero temperatures. One memorable year someone in London got it wrong and after a long delay the entire Embassy order arrived in January – frozen solid! Corks had been forced off bottles with such force that they had gone through the thick cardboard cases, and some bottles had cracked leaving alcoholic, bottle-shaped ice lollies!

Chapter Three: Diplomatic Life

The lives of diplomats in Beijing were completely regulated, some went as far as to say governed, by the Chinese Diplomatic Services Bureau (DSB). They allocated certain flats to certain Embassies and they alone appointed staff: be it secretary, cook or driver you were never allowed the privilege of interviewing or choosing employees, you simply took whoever they sent you. So it was that at 8.30 the morning after we'd arrived in Beijing, Mrs. Yuan turned up on our doorstep. We'd said before leaving the U.K. that the whole concept of servants was alien to us and we'd be happier without any, but it appeared that we'd been 'issued' with one anyway. Mike asked her what exactly her duties were and she explained that she did all the washing, ironing and cleaning while the *'furen'* (lady of the house) sat and drank coffee with all the other wives. She also explained that we were to call her *'ayi'*, which literally meant 'auntie' but was a term of address for all female servants. Sadly, the vast majority of foreigners used the term in a somewhat derogatory manner as the old colonial 'boy', so we insisted that we would refer to her by her name as a mark of the respect she was due. She adored children, and a good gossip, as much as she really didn't enjoy cleaning, so we soon arrived at a happy compromise: she babysat and ironed to perfection, I washed and cleaned, and any other jobs we tackled together while she taught me colloquial Chinese. I also refused to keep to the 'rules' as regards her working hours: many ayis weren't allowed home a moment before 5.30, even if they'd finished all their work and were just sitting in the kitchen watching the clock. This rather unconventional working arrangement was frowned upon by many, but it suited us: Mrs. Yuan would have done anything for us, as we would have done to help her, and she became as close to us as a member of our own family.

When we returned to Beijing for the second time we were allowed to have Mrs. Yuan as our ayi again, but as the children were then of school age, and we often had to travel on Naval visits we realised that, alien as the concept was to us, we needed an English speaking nanny. The British Foreign Office rules however, stated that if you employed a nanny, you also had to have two other members of 'staff'. This was sensibly to protect the nanny from being used as an au pair and expected to do household chores as well as childcare. Our choices were limited to either a driver or a cook, and as we both loved driving, we opted for the latter. Enter Mr. Zhang, sent by the DSB. He was young and inexperienced (he used to cook rice at the Egyptian Embassy), but the only one that could be found who didn't smoke (we had insisted on that). He was very willing to learn and soon was producing the most delicious meals for us and our guests. There was never a problem as long as your instructions were clear: unlike one wife who wanted her cook to serve Baked Alaska at a dinner party – "you just put icecream and fruit over the sponge, top with the egg whites and put into a hot oven", only she had forgotten to tell him to first beat the egg whites!

The DSB functioned not only as a way of organising our lives, but as a protector of the local employees. We were warned by fellow diplomats that we would undoubtedly lose our ayi if she appeared to be getting too friendly and therefore too 'westernised', which probably did happen on occasion, but there was another side to the coin: should an ayi's life be made unbearably miserable by one family, the DSB could move her without giving either notice or explanation. In the summer of 1983, I invited Mrs. Yuan to go on holiday with me and the children to the seaside resort of Beidaihe: she had never been and was delighted. I mentioned my plan to another mother who said that when she had tried to do the same, the DSB had not allowed the ayi to live in the diplomatic guest rooms, but insisted she sleep in the Chinese dormitory. Full of fury and righteous indignation I prepared to do battle, but Mrs. Yuan asked around and told me what had really happened. The ayi concerned had been consulted as to whether she wanted to stay 'with the foreigners', and she was adamant that she didn't. Not that she had anything against them, but could see herself being in charge of the children 24 hours a day instead of the usual 8. Mrs. Yuan was allowed to have her own bedroom next to mine and we had a wonderful holiday even though we had to pay her extra wages. In Beijing she was an ayi and paid as such, at Beidaihe she was classed as a guide and they earned more – quite amazing when you considered that my 'guide' had never been there before and it was my third visit! (Mind you, she certainly earned the guide's salary with her sourcing fresh crabs and arranging with the kitchen to steam them for us).

A very large number of expats. were firmly convinced that all household employees were spies, searching for anything which might incriminate you and so be used against you. Whilst about their spying they were supposedly not above stealing the odd item that took their fancy – anything from thermos flask stoppers to "knickers and nail varnish". Should anything go missing it was always assumed that 'They' had taken it. In all our time in China 'They' never bothered us - maybe my underwear wasn't exotic enough, and I didn't paint my nails anyway, or maybe our bank statements were such as to evoke only sympathy, but we never found any evidence that anything of ours had been stolen or even disturbed. Mind you, it was a standing joke about the electronic bugging devices that may well have been present in all our flats: the chances were they broke down pretty fast, but on the off-chance that they were in use, we took advantage of them to suggest ways of improving the flats, shops etc. or to complain that something wasn't working. If action was taken within a couple of days (which it often was, maybe purely coincidentally) we'd look at each other and say "They've been listening again".

There was only one occasion when we felt that maybe someone was walking not too far behind, and that was when we were accosted in a park by a very harmless, but very mentally deficient young man. Unable to understand a word he said we kept walking, with him at our side. Unobtrusively, and without a word spoken, a man quickened his pace to catch up with us, gently but firmly linked his arm through that of our companion, and led him away along another path. This mild surveillance was more comforting than oppressive: it would have been impossible to get lost if you wandered off the beaten track. On a visit to the Summer Palace, some miles outside the city, we once locked the keys inside the car. By the time we had discovered what we had done it was late afternoon so we arranged a lift home and decided to return for the car the following day. Within minutes of our entering the flat the phone rang; it was the Embassy saying that they had had the Public Security Bureau on the phone wondering why we had abandoned our car, and were we safely home, or locked in the Palace for the night!

Some countries were so worried about being spied on that they employed no Chinese people in their homes. It was rather disconcerting at times to be served a drink at an Attaché's flat by a giant bear of a security guard whose hand completely encompassed the proffered glass and who could have crushed the same (or an assailant's ribs!) with the ease of a mere mortal crushing paper. Probably the most insular of all Embassies was the Soviet one: situated some miles distant from the other diplomatic areas it was almost a town in its own right, housing all Russian residents, shop, school, sports facilities and, it was rumoured, a small hospital. Twice a year, if we were on diplomatic terms, we entered the walled enclave; once we were delivered by Embassy car to attend a reception in a large, chandelier-bedecked hall, and once to attend the annual Canada v. Russia ice hockey match, held on a specially frozen-over pitch. The latter event, being less formal, allowed us to drive our own car there, and we arrived at one of the many gates to find it firmly shut and not a soul in sight. Sitting in the car and debating what to do, we noticed the gates very slowly glide open: although we could see nobody, they were obviously watching us. It was from the Russians, in fact, that we had most of the feeling of being watched while we were in China. Very shortly after our arrival we were wandering around the Friendship Store and we were stopped by a couple of about our age, also with two small children. The man introduced himself as the Deputy Russian Military Attaché, his wife as a teacher of English and his children as prospective good friends for ours, whose names he somehow knew without our telling him! Throughout our stay we saw them from time to time: he would be obliged to call on Mike at regular intervals, presumably just so he could say he had fulfilled his mission, even though he never had anything worthy of reporting. Even Mike's ploy of trying to find the coldest/hottest, least inviting venue in the Embassy failed to deter him from his statutory one hour. She was a pleasant enough woman, probably a good teacher, but admitted that she really didn't like children – at least not her own. As the children grew older, she tried always to arrange for one of them to be staying in Moscow with granny. It was a source of great amusement to see their return to Beijing for a second tour of duty at the same time as us, especially as we had adopted another child in the interim and they had, we surmised, been told to match up: this reluctant mother had produced another baby! One Christmas they gave us a beautiful set of Babushka stacking dolls for the children, and some very upmarket Russian chocolates for Mike and I. Our underlying, and in this case totally unfounded, suspicion of anything 'Soviet' meant that I tried one chocolate and we waited one day until Mike tried one! Too many 'spy' films with truth drugs etc.!!

As foreigners we were quite severely restricted as to where we could go and who we could talk to, although we fared better as Diplomats than the business community, who had a very hard time on occasion. Driving our own cars was permitted, but only within the city; a limit of 20km was imposed, and except to visit the Great Wall, Ming Tombs or airport we were not allowed beyond without special permission. On every road leading out of Beijing a notice was erected at the 20km point stating, in English, Russian and Chinese, that foreigners were not allowed to proceed without such permission. Should we wish to visit another city, such as Shanghai, a written application had first to be lodged with the Public Security Bureau, stating date and duration of visit and the reason for it. After due, and often lengthy, deliberation, permission would be granted – or refused. To be correct, it was never refused; the visit was just declared to be 'inconvenient'. This phrase we came to meet many times and in many different contexts, and it was very hard to argue with: you had not been refused your request, just put off – probably indefinitely. Far from finding this an annoyance, we turned it into a game – if we read about a festival or particularly scenic area we would ask for clearance to go there. We were given permission quite often, and a sheaf of papers was issued which was inspected with great frequency throughout the journey. There were two probable reasons for the refusal of a request: national security and personal safety. Military Attachés were obviously thought to be something of a risk on the first count: they were on the whole suspected of being would-be spies, and so we were watched very carefully if anywhere near a 'sensitive' area. It was not unusual for one's itinerary to be suddenly changed if there was thought to be any risk of your seeing something 'unsuitable' (such as military or naval movements): on a visit to Nanjing our return flight was 'cancelled' and we spent the day, in the pouring rain, wandering around a rather depressed zoo and admiring the famous bridge – only the visibility was so poor I couldn't tell you to this day what it looked like. Seats were found for us on a flight which took off after dark, and our suspicions were confirmed when we arrived at the airport and were quizzed as to why we had failed to turn up in the morning for the flight which – surprise, surprise – hadn't been cancelled at all. As regards your personal wellbeing the authorities were positively paranoid that something untoward might happen to you for which they would be held responsible. Upon arrival at your destination you were met by a guide (for which you had to pay) who would stick to you like glue and organise your visit. It was occasionally possible to say where you wanted to go, but on the whole the hassle wasn't worth it.

Even after the more 'open door' policy reigned, there still remained a fear of responsibility for visitors. When Mike was lecturing at a Naval establishment, he was issued with a bodyguard – although no one seemed to know what he was to guard against. Even a relaxing mountain walk between lectures necessitated the accompaniment of a doctor and a nurse struggling behind, carrying medical bags and resuscitation kit!

Attachés were given six weeks' grace to settle in, unpack etc. before the hectic social whirl hit them – and the pace never slackened until the moment you left. Every country represented had a National Day, Independence Day or the like, and many also celebrated Armed Forces Day, the ruler's birthday etc. and for each event a cocktail party would be held, the format of which never changed. Starting on the dot of either 1 or 6 pm you would arrive at the Embassy concerned and begin by filing past the welcome committee of Ambassador and senior Attachés and their wives, shaking hands with each one. Passing into the reception room you would fight your way through the crowd until you reached the Military Attachés and their wives, who would be standing in adjoining yet distinctly separate, groups. A sort of 'his and hers' party. Mike would then break off and shake hands with each wife in turn, while I did the same with their husbands, whereupon we would change places and I would greet the wives by kissing them on both cheeks. (Mike stuck to shaking hands with the men, although some were into hugging.) Care had to be taken even in this seemingly simple exercise, as some religious beliefs forbade the touching of women. The following hour would be spent in small talk within your 'group', punctuated by waiters offering drinks and canapés, until the senior guests started to leave and you followed suit. Transport to these receptions was always by way of an Embassy car, and it became a point of honour among the drivers to time their arrival at the door to coincide with the exact moment of your exit. This must have entailed all manner of manoeuvring of vehicles, usually in very restricted spaces, but our particular driver never failed. The undisputed 'king', however, was 'Speedy', the British Ambassador's driver, who could leave for a function after the rest of us and yet always arrive first.

During your tour of duty you aimed to entertain every other Military Attaché at least once, and the majority of them changed every three years – so that made a lot of dinner parties. These dinners were almost as formal as the receptions, and the rituals of greeting and sitting in one-sex groups remained the same, but what you did gain was the opportunity of sampling food from all over the world and it never once disappointed. After the first few of these culinary experiences, I realised that it was essential to take very small portions, as you would be urged most vehemently to partake of a second helping and if you refused it would be taken as an indication that you didn't like the food. For the most part these dinner parties were very enjoyable, but once or twice they proved to be really hard going – when your fellow guests all turned out to be non-English speakers, or if you had exhausted all conversation at the one or even two cocktails you had attended that same day! Some Attachés overcame this by showing films after the dinner – ranging from 'Airplane' to famous Belly Dancers – while one Burmese wife developed the unique ability to fall asleep the instant she had taken her last mouthful and snored gently until awakened by the sound of guests leaving. Whether indulging in small talk, animated conversation, or watching a film, the dinner would last exactly two and a half hours, whereupon, Cinderella-like, all the guests would leave. If you weren't allowed to stay longer, nor were you allowed to depart earlier; no one would move until the most senior Attaché present (i.e. the one who had been in China longest) stood up and said his goodbyes. The only time I ever saw any variation to this strict timetable was one evening when we were entertaining in the older of the two flats we occupied: shortly after the dinner, two large mice suddenly ran out into the middle of the floor and started a vicious fight, totally unperturbed by our presence. On that occasion no one objected to a slightly early departure – not the wives at any rate.

Less frequent social occasions were drinks parties, usually held at the International Club or, in later years, at hotels, to welcome new arrivals and bid farewell to their predecessors. These followed the same format as other events except that the Dean of the Attaché Corps gave a speech and a presentation was made. For many years the Dean was a Rumanian: he had been in Beijing for as long as anyone could remember and always made the same speech, ending with the customary bouquet for the departing wife and the immortal words "and to the wife a bunch of flowers for good behaviour". One African Attaché rather confused the issue by having four wives, although only two accompanied him to China at any one time, the other two staying behind with the many children. Every six months they would change roles and countries, so if you invited the Attaché to dinner you had no idea which of the four would be with him, although they were all equally charming. Upon his departure a larger than usual bouquet was presented "for the family".

We thoroughly enjoyed the company of our fellow Attachés and wives, but the friendly, relaxed atmosphere could sadly alter overnight should Diplomatic Relations be broken off between our government and another. The worst time was the occasion of the Falklands War when we were suddenly not permitted to talk to our very dear Argentinian friends. Mike quite naturally had to comply but I considered that a wife on neutral territory was less constricted, so continued to talk at social functions if not privately. I felt that to be particularly important at the time, as their eldest daughter had just been admitted to hospital with an undiagnosed stomach disorder. (She recovered, and the illness was put down to a surfeit of under-ripe plums!). There was a story recounted, the veracity of which I cannot guarantee, of one Ambassador being directed by his government to make a 'high level' complaint to another Ambassador. He did as instructed: upon entering the office, he climbed onto the desk and said "I complain, from this high level". They, being good friends, then sat together and talked through the problem between their two governments.

Just sometimes someone would get it all wrong – and it happened a few times to me. Being very new to the Diplomatic life it was perhaps understandable that I assumed the guest from the PLO was part of an orchestra rather than a political organisation. And there was no way of telling that the Chinese 'guests' I was talking to were in fact the cleaners sneaking a look at the party. The worst 'faux pas' I shared with the Canadian Attaché's wife when we both turned up to an Arab 'men only' cocktail party – we braved it out, but kept a low profile in a corner of the garden. (As her husband said, we were making the point that women should have been invited). The worst disaster was one that nearly happened, but fortunately didn't. One particular Attaché always sported the most ornate and extremely smart uniform which was much admired by all, until he received notice of the impending official visit of his Chief of Staff. Frantic telephone calls had to be made home – not to ensure a successful visit, but to order a new uniform. When asked by friends what was wrong with his smart and new-looking one he admitted that he had had it made locally to his own design as he always thought the real one so dull compared with those of his colleagues.

The other 'side' to an Attaché's social life was with The People's Liberation Army, The People's Liberation Army Navy or The People's

Liberation Army Air Force – yes they do have those titles! In fact, the only military personnel that we were allowed contact with were all of a special section called the Foreign Affairs Bureau (FAB) who, although they had once been in active service, were all office-based. Our first meeting with the Chinese Navy was at a banquet held to welcome Mike (as the first British Naval Attaché since his predecessor left in the Amethyst), and we soon learnt that banquets, like cocktail parties, had a set format. The most important point was to arrive exactly on time (usually 6.30) and to achieve this objective you planned with your driver to arrive about ten minutes early and then drive round the block a few times or park round the corner. At the precise moment for which you were invited, you were met and ushered in to an anteroom, the walls of which were lined with large armchairs sporting lace antimacassars, with low coffee tables in front. The Chinese host and most important guest were ushered into the central position, flanked by interpreters, while the rest occupied the remaining chairs, and tea was served. Even if the foreign guest spoke perfect Chinese, an interpreter was always used for conversation between himself and his host – this was partly to avoid any possibility of misunderstanding, but primarily to give everyone 'thinking time' to formulate a reply while the interpreter was talking. Whilst the initial pleasantries were being exchanged the waitresses were in constant attendance topping up tea cups – beware: Chinese tea, whilst being delicious and very refreshing, is also diuretic! After five or ten minutes we all moved into the dining room and took our allotted places at a round table, in the centre of which was a revolving circular platform laid out with dishes of cold hors d'oeuvres. These were followed by course upon delicious course until we felt we'd never eat again, all washed down with glasses of either fizzy orange, mineral water, red wine that tasted like a mixture of port and cough medicine, or maotai. This fiery liquor is made from sorghum and the best description I came across was that it tasted like tom cats! If drunk correctly you didn't in fact taste it very much, as the small glassfuls were supposed to be downed in one to cries of 'ganbei' ('dry glass'). Hardened banqueters – and the Chinese Navy boasted not a few – could down an amazing number and expected guests to match them. Assurances that it didn't 'go to your head' might have been true, but it could certainly hit your stomach pretty hard, and all manner of tricks were instituted by foreigners wishing to preserve their livers, such as not swallowing your mouthful and spitting it into your orange drink in the pretence of sipping it; swapping glasses etc. No matter how well tried and tested the ruse, few of us escaped many a hangover. At about half-way through the meal speeches were made, during which it was not only considered rude to speak, but to eat as well. A banquet would normally last about one and a half hours, when the host would suddenly announce, apropos of nothing, "you must be tired". The first time we heard this we naturally disagreed (it was after all only 8 pm), but soon came to realise that it was just a verbal signal that the banquet was over. The Chinese didn't go in for prolonged farewells either – a quick handshake and a word of farewell and you were speeding your way home.

Banquets were very lavish affairs, undoubtedly very costly and probably quite wasteful, until one day the government issued an edict that they should be scaled down to a more realistic level of expenditure. The very expensive maotai was gradually replaced by Chinese wine which, through a joint venture with France, proved to be perfectly acceptable to all but the connoisseur. Fourteen courses were cut to six or seven, but often still punctuated mid-banquet with slices of sponge cake liberally covered in bright green buttercream icing, or even jam sandwiches: I think, like sorbet, it was meant to cleanse the palate. An even cheaper alternative, especially if a large number of guests was involved, was to host a buffet supper. These proved to be less popular, as there was little opportunity for serious discussion, standing up, balancing plate and glass and being jostled and distracted by other guests. For some reason I was never able to fathom, should your Chinese host have a matter of some importance to convey to you, or a particular favour to ask, it would never be mentioned until the very end of the meal, giving very little time for discussion before "you must be tired". Perhaps it was a 'throwback' to old Chinese etiquette when, even if you were in great pain, you wouldn't think of telling your doctor until the full half hour or more of polite pleasantries and enquiries about his family had been voiced. Buffets also seemed to confuse the Chinese at first, who didn't seem to grasp the concept of returning to the food several times, but would pile everything onto their plates at once: salads, meats, fish, gravies, cakes, fruit, ice cream etc. all mingled together. Not too many years previously there had been a serious famine in many parts of the country, so perhaps it was the sight of so much food that made them desperate not to miss out on anything – that would at least be one explanation as to why they also stuffed their pockets full with bread rolls to take home (better than wasting them, anyway).

Whatever the type of meal, we were always invited to a restaurant or hotel, never to the host's home – it would have been seen to reflect badly on their standard of living compared with ours in the West. The irony was that their homes were not so very different from our own in the U.K., whilst in Beijing we were housed to a degree that even Homes and Gardens would have envied. Surprisingly we never once encountered any show of resentment of our comparatively palatial home, either from official visitors or ayis. We were quite free to invite members of the FAB and Naval Officers to our flat, but could only suggest which guests we would like, the final decision being made by the hierarchy. It was quite interesting to see who turned up, as they wouldn't let you know in advance. Over the years, and with increased trust in certain foreigners, these rather formal dinners became more relaxed. We eventually dispensed with the hiring of waiters if we invited friends from the Chinese Navy, finding the atmosphere far better if we all 'mucked in' together in passing plates etc. Probably the greatest compliment we were paid as regards acceptance was the evening when some of our guests felt comfortable enough to arrive early rather than wait outside, and set to laying the table and helping the children with their homework. One of them told me that many years in the past it was obligatory to arrive very early for a dinner as a sign of great eagerness at the prospect of dining with your host, but it was also necessary to leave long before the meal had finished to show that you had been so well fed that you couldn't even contemplate looking upon another dish. Fortunately our guests stayed until the end – and beyond.

Over the years relations became more relaxed and in February 1987 all Naval Attachés were invited by the Chinese Navy to a Spring Festival Party at the Foreign Affairs Bureau. The buffet supper was second to none and was followed by a summons to the 'ballroom' – for 'Foreign Friends' liked to dance. The Navy band played – and not a soul moved. Encouragements were spoken over the loudspeaker – still no response: if the Attachés were waiting for the Dean to make the first move they waited in vain. The situation was getting extremely embarrassing: the Chinese had tried to lay on the kind of party we'd undoubtedly enjoy and it was turning into an absolute disaster. With one thought Mike and I made for the floor and started to dance the nearest to a waltz we could manage, but two people hardly make a party so we homed in on the Attaché we knew would never allow himself to be shown up by the British. Our hunch proved correct – with very little persuasion the Russian and his wife were on their feet and dancing, closely followed by the majority of the other Attachés, but sadly not by our Chinese hosts. Dancing had been frowned upon for so long that they had lost the knack.

That the party had been deemed a success, and that our hosts felt the desire to participate more fully, was evidenced the following year when the second Spring Festival Party was held. When the time came to repair to the ballroom there were present a large number of Chinese lady Naval personnel who, together with their male counterparts, had obviously spent a large part of the previous year at dancing lessons. They soon put us all to shame with their proficient and often complicated routines and manoeuvres, and were clearly enjoying every minute of the more relaxed atmosphere.

This apparent relaxation in the strict rules governing relations between foreigners and Chinese allowed us to visit, with a mutual, non-diplomatic friend, a young artist employed by the Beijing Puppet Troupe. Born and brought up in Beijing and aware of its rapid modernisation, he specialised in oil paintings of the old city which would one day be gone forever. Being used to painting backdrops, his pictures were so lifelike as to appear almost photographic. His tiny two room flat (living room and tiny bedroom – shared toilet on the landing) was in a dilapidated building with cracked concrete stairs and lightbulbs missing on many of the communal landings, which were also used as storage places for numerous boxes and bicycles. Canvases were stacked in every available space: wonderful scenes of town and country, plus one very fine portrait of a young Chinese peasant girl, but the talent totally wasted as there was no way he could market what we knew would be popular paintings, so we organised an exhibition and sale for himself and some fellow artists to be held in our flat. It was a great success – several paintings were sold and genuine interest shown by all the invited guests: we felt we had started them on the path to some recognition and success. A few months later a letter was circulated to all foreign residents stating that it was, from that day, illegal to hold art exhibitions in Embassies or private residences! Angered and frustrated, we had no choice, as guests in the country, but to abide by their rules, and could only be grateful that we had managed to purchase so many vivid pictorial mementos. About seven or eight months later we received a request, through a third party, to host a cocktail party at an hotel we'd never even heard of, to the west of the city. The party would just happen to coincide with an exhibition of paintings in the same room. After some consideration we agreed: it was not, after all, to be held in our 'private residence'. On that occasion it was, sadly, not the authorities who put the seal of disaster on the affair, but the artists themselves. Somewhere along the line greed had reared its ugly head and we were totally shocked to find their prices had trebled or even quadrupled, which was more than just annoying, it was embarrassing for us as we had told our invited guests the range of prices they might expect to pay for these works. Needless to say, they sold not a single painting and although we remained good friends, we never again volunteered to help them: they had spoilt it for themselves.

Chapter Four: Entertainment

Before discos, clubs and video rentals arrived in China, which they inevitably did, there was very little in the way of entertainment, and it was especially sparse for foreign residents.

As in most homes across the world, television was the most popular medium and as such was used, in the 80s at least, as a means of conveying the 'Party Line'. Programmes, with the exception of an occasional documentary about another region of China, were full of Communist ideals and not-so-subtle propaganda. When we, back home, would have been watching 'Soaps' here we had 'Electricity Part 13: electromagnetic force' followed by 'Radio for Amateurs: simple measuring of transistors'. Prime time slots were occupied by documentaries extolling the virtues of great military leaders or great Party members, or films about love of family and Country conquering all. The news featured a great number of reports of wonderful increases of food production by 'model' communes. Sometimes a criminal trial would be reported on, the accused, head shaved and in manacles being roughly forced by two policemen to bow to the Court. Further footage showed a police van driving out into the country to the execution site. There was little light relief in the adverts either, which mostly featured tractors and heavy machinery.

Over the years a news bulletin in English appeared, along with more drama (although always moralistic), but the finer points of presenting were still missing: just as the final programme of the day was ending, a disembodied voice would say an abrupt "goodnight" and transmission would end – no music, no "thank you for watching", just an instant blank screen. This would often be as early as 10.30, as everyone went to bed and arose much earlier than we were used to.

Theatre was a less frequented source of entertainment, but an extremely good one. For foreigners the difficulty was in finding out what was on and where (the later publication of The China Daily newspaper in English helped a lot), and in getting tickets. There was no system where you could telephone a box office or the like; your only hope was to go to the theatre a few days in advance and hang around, often for hours, until someone turned up who would sell tickets.

There was a reasonable variety of shows, although the Revolutionary Operas of the time of Chairman Mao had ceased to be on the repertoire. Traditional, and beautifully costumed, dramas of maidens in distress and lovers parted, could be seen together with the well-known Peking Opera. "A group of arguing tomcats" or "an untuned orchestra" were but two of the many comments I often heard about this particular art form, for the music seemed totally alien to the Western ear. In addition to which the songs were given a unique intonation which made them incomprehensible even to many Chinese members of the audience, so the words, in Chinese characters, were projected on to screens at either side of the stage. I personally loved the sound, but to the majority of foreigners it was purely the visual spectacle that made it worthy of a visit, for the costumes must have been amongst the most opulent ever seen: rich colours with intricate embroidery, elaborate headdresses that seemed to defy gravity, triangular flags protruding from the shoulders – it was amazing that the performers were so agile. Many of the actors also wore very detailed facial makeup resembling masks which were symbolic as well as colourful: a red face denoted bravery; a black one honesty and justice; a white one treachery and a yellow one ruthlessness, and even within these parameters an expert could tell the age and disposition of a character through subtle differences in the makeup.

Stories of the renowned Monkey King were also loosely labelled 'opera', but had a good deal of the circus in them, featuring as they did amazing acrobatics and split-second timing with hurtling spears. One female performer I saw could return spears and staffs thrown to her not just with her hands, but by kicking back ones thrown from the rear – and without once turning her head to look. This athleticism and timing must have been partly inborn as I often saw young children in the street tossing heavy-based shuttlecocks into the air for minutes on end and using only the sides of their feet.

The best way for a foreigner to enjoy Peking Opera was to attend a performance containing excerpts from several operas – a whole evening of one opera could be very tedious, but even then many foreigners failed to see the best performances simply because they left the theatre before the end.   This was understandable if your tour followed the usual timetable: Great Wall, Ming Tombs, hurried dinner and the opera. Tired at the start and subjected to an earbashing of unintelligible and seemingly unmelodious songs, few decided not to leave and retreat to their hotels for an early night. This was wonderful for the locals (and me!) as they could only afford the cheaper seats at the back, but once the second half had begun and it was obvious the 'foreign friends' were not planning to return, there was a great scrabbling and rushing to occupy the first few rows.   The most colourful, acrobatic and impressive performance was always saved till last but was, sadly, missed by many.

Far more popular and a 'must' for all visitors was The Railway Workers Acrobatic Troupe which, despite the name, was not made up of talented engine drivers, linesmen and engineers but was a group of highly professional entertainers sponsored, and employed, by the Railway Workers. Their acrobatic performances were the best I have ever seen: unbelievably complicated balancing acts involving tables, chairs, trays of glasses; little girls who could bend their bodies into positions that seemed to defy anatomical possibility; jugglers throwing very large and heavy ceramic pots and catching them effortlessly on shoulders or heads – each act seemed more amazing than the last, culminating with the traditional 'Lion Dance'.

Whereas acrobatics, musical dramas and opera could be found on somewhere all year round, an occasional visitor was the circus – sometimes performed in a sports stadium, sometimes in the traditional 'Big Top' erected on a spare piece of ground (increasingly hard to find in the city). The circus was without exception run by a very small group who did everything from selling tickets and sweeping up to performing, and the standards ranged from professional to extremely amateur. One lady bareback rider missed her cue every time and instead of leaping gracefully onto the horse's back repeatedly landed with an undignified and undoubtedly painful thump on her bottom on the hard floor. While that was going on, another performer was agilely dodging the horse's hooves in an attempt to hack away (with a very blunt knife) a potentially dangerous loop of rope that had suddenly appeared through the sawdust. The whole performance was further punctuated from my point of view (or lack of!) by a team of incredibly tall American basketball players who had obviously had a few beers beforehand and one after the other, at intervals of a few minutes apart, had to work their way along the rows to go to the toilet.

The most frightening performance I ever saw at a circus involved tigers. A circular cage had been erected in the ring, but a large number of the bolts fastening the sections together were missing and I was sure that if one of the animals threw itself against the bars the whole cage would have collapsed leaving tigers on the loose. I spent most of the performance working out whether it would be best to run for the only exit or hide under the seats!

Whatever the type of entertainment the common denominator was desperately hard and uncomfortable seating and smelly toilets. Even the more upmarket theatres boasted little more luxury than thin carpet laid on top of the concrete floor. There were a couple of other noticeable differences between theatre in China and theatre as we know it. The first was a matter of logistics: seats were numbered with number one being in the middle and all seats to the left being even numbers and all those to the right being odd. There were also two entrances to the auditorium, marked 'odd' and 'even' – in Chinese characters. This caused great confusion and sometimes consternation amongst the foreigners who would find that seats 35 and 36 were at opposite ends of the same row.

The second difference was the attitude of a Chinese audience. A night out was a great event to be enjoyed to the full and if eating, drinking tea, knitting or whispering comments to neighbours enhanced this enjoyment then it was quite acceptable to do any or all of these things during a performance. On one occasion a visiting conductor was invited to take part in a concert but was amazed that no matter how many times nor how insistently he tapped his baton and raised his arms in expectation of silence, absolutely nothing happened. The rustling, chewing, clicking of knitting needles etc. continued unabated, but be assured that once he finally gave up and the orchestra started to play anyway, the audience was not one jot less appreciative of the music than their counterparts at the Albert Hall. If they didn't feel it essential to their enjoyment to remain utterly still and silent, by the same token they didn't turn a hair when overhead floodlights suddenly exploded and showered them with fragments of glass. They just brushed the glass onto the floor and the performance continued without a hiccough.

Any change in the comfort and modernisation of theatres was slow to come about, but restrictions on foreign performers were relaxed by the late 80s to an extent I would not have thought possible. One particular visiting dance troupe's repertoire contained a modern ballet performed by six men as elements of 'fire'. It would best be described as a competition to see who could pour himself into the tightest leotard and still move – they might just as well have danced naked! And no one will ever convince me that the party of young men next to me were interested in the artistic talents of the daringly dressed female performers! To ensure that any visiting overseas troupes performed to a full house, any unsold tickets were often given to the local army camp and soldiers sent along to fill the seats. I imagine once word got around of this new, more liberal attitude, they were never short of volunteers to attend.

There were undoubtedly a few other theatrical events and films on offer, but none that we normally ever heard about or which would have been intelligible to us, so any other entertainment was self-generated within the expatriate community. For the socialites there was TGIF held at different Embassies on a rota system, and if enough musical talent was found recitals were organised, often in the British Ambassador's Residence. No room could have been more suited to listening to music than the Sitting Room, with its classical decor, piano and large wall-hanging tapestry whose colours had faded over the years to a muted hue.

Our Amenities Hall also saw occasional discos, dances and, in the days before videos, film shows. Two I remember in particular: the ballet version of 'The Tales of Beatrix Potter' which somewhat confused the Chinese ballet students present, and a James Bond film Mike screened for the Military Attachés. At the time we were not on diplomatic terms with the Russians so they were not invited, but managed to hear about it and gatecrashed. Not wanting to create an unnecessary incident Mike allowed them to stay and greeted them as if they were expected. I can't remember the name of the film, but by pure chance it featured a large number of stereotypical Russians – hefty KGB men, all brute force and ignorance – who were easily outwitted by Bond and mercilessly dealt embarrassing ends. Our gatecrashers left at the interval without a word. Other Embassies periodically screened films with as varied contents as travelogues (all blue skies, flowers and mountains); graphic war scenes (all bloody bodies and bits of bodies), and – best of all – E.T.

A lack of 'laid on' entertainment was in many ways an advantage, especially at Christmas time. No sale of gifts and cards as early as September, no bombardment of adverts for toys, and no hours of television (the sort you feel you can't miss, but so quickly forget afterwards). Everything was as it used to be years ago, from the children's parties to carol singing in that wonderful room at the Residence. On Christmas morning we would all gather at the Amenities Hall for our own service of lessons and carols (everyone's favourites included!) followed by sherry and mince pies. As it wasn't a Chinese holiday many people would hire a cook for the day and upon their return from the service they would be greeted by the smell of roasting turkey with as many of the traditional trimmings as they'd managed to accumulate from the Embassy shop or a visit to Hong Kong. It was certainly true that your appreciation increased in direct proportion to the difficulty in obtaining any item. Boxing Day was the one time every year when the entire British community (Embassy personnel, businessmen, teachers, students etc.) would meet together socially, and it was by tradition on the frozen Summer Palace lake, for flasks of hot toddy, skating, sledging and, to the total amazement of the locals, cricket on ice.

One of the high spots of the entertainment scene at that time of year was undoubtedly the Embassy Pantomime – such gems as 'Robin and the Forty Thieves' and 'Jack and the Beansprouts'. It was amazing what talent there was to be found in this moving population, not just in acting, singing and dancing, but in the writing of the very amusing and witty script, which managed to appeal to children and adults alike. The authors managed a perfect balance of the essential elements of slapstick – lots of the old favourite "it's behind you" and "oh yes he is" – and extremely clever but good-natured digs at local conditions. In one performance a disinterested 'Chinese' airline clerk whose entire vocabulary seemed to consist of the words "not convenient" and "meiyou", was seated at a desk behind which was hanging, crookedly, the airline motto 'We Serve You Right'. (I did actually once see a large sign just outside Canton airport welcoming visitors with the immortal words 'You're Welcome To China').

By the time of our return to Beijing in 1986 Amusement Parks had arrived – two to be exact. Similar in the 'rides' offered, the number not working and my mistrust of their safety inspections and maintenance, they were nevertheless a great source of enjoyment to us and to Chinese families, especially as one of them would take Renminbi. Highlights were a 'log ride' with small, yet very wetting, water chute; a good old-fashioned roundabout complete with painted horses; a 'monorail' which you pedalled around a track some 20 feet above the ground, and a maze created not with hedges but with bamboo canes. Because you could see through these bamboo 'walls' it appeared to be easy to work out your route, but the mass of slanting, interwoven canes played amazing tricks on your eyes and it was harder than any conventional maze I had ever seen. The most popular of the amusements for Jonathan, then aged 7, was the go-carts, and it was amazing to see him complete the course with no trouble while Chinese youths of three times his age were crashing into the barriers at every turn – and sometimes even on the straight! The reason for this was that he had the great advantage of having spent many hours as a passenger watching and, as all young boys, emulating the driver, whereas the majority of the locals had probably only been in a taxi a few times, if at all, and relied entirely on buses or bicycles.

For the extremely wealthy, and therefore almost exclusively foreign, residents, golf had also arrived and courses were appearing in the countryside around Beijing. I would have thought the charges prohibitive but it was reportedly cheaper for a Japanese golfer to fly to China for a round than to play in his own country.

As for television, the viewing hours extended later into the evening and a few 'soaps' (still very moralistic) appeared, but there was still nothing of outstanding interest – except the one programme in which Anna appeared.

The Chinese Television Company were putting on the biggest Spring Festival extravaganza ever staged, hosted by the famed Zhang Kun (the Terry Wogan of Beijing) and required two foreign children to take part in one of the many acts: Anna had been asked through a teacher at the International School together with a French boy from their school, and a local Chinese girl. They were to take part in a sketch about a child's birthday party and a money box. Despite the many comic lines, the basic moral of saving money (preferably with the sponsoring bank!) came across loud and clear.

Filming was to take place at an hotel near the Ming Tombs, and we arrived with Anna (who had previously learned her Chinese lines) at the appointed time of 10.30am to be shown into a comfortable lounge area adjacent to the ballroom and served soft drinks. Anna was needed 'on set' at 11.30 and we were invited to make ourselves at home and "rest awhile". The hour came and went, only punctuated every ten minutes or so by someone putting his head around the door and encouraging us to "rest awhile". By 12.30 we felt we had rested quite enough – we had no books, drawing paper, games for the children and we were *all* feeling very bored. At last we were summoned, but not to start filming but to have lunch; a very tasty meal shared with a girl who juggled with her feet and a comedian. Assuring our hosts that we had indeed eaten well and sufficiently, we hoped to get on with the show as it were but our expectations were dashed when we were ushered into a guest room of the hotel where there were two beds, a television and a bathroom, and where we might better "rest awhile". It was 'siesta' time for the Chinese, so no hope of anything moving for a couple of hours, so when in Rome... The afternoon drifted by, but at least we had television and we went for a walk around the small grounds of the hotel to relieve the boredom, until at last we were collected. A quick run-through of Anna's lines, a brush of her hair and off we went – to the restaurant for dinner! By that time we were having serious doubts that we had maybe gone on the wrong day, especially as yet another "rest" was to be had after we'd eaten, but at last, at 10 o'clock in the evening we were summoned (perhaps we'd muddled am with pm). For the first time we met the other two children - not at their best either as although they'd not waited nearly as long as we had, the French boy kept falling asleep. They were taken off for a quick rehearsal and makeup, while Anna's younger brother Tom kept the rest of us amused by throwing up all over the floor, which fortunately wasn't carpeted.

Finally ready to go, except Zhang Kun wasn't, so we all moved to another room bedecked in lights, backdrops and plastic grape vines to watch him complete the filming of a 5 minute comedy sketch, whereupon it was back to the ballroom we'd first seen those many hours before. Whilst the audience were rearranged so that the best dressed and most attractive were at the front, a team of electricians dismantled all the lights, but fortunately not the plastic grapes, from the other room and rewired them ready for use. I never did discover why they didn't just use one room for all the filming. The sponsoring bank's large logo was ceremoniously hoisted into a prominent position mid camera shot, the actors assembled and the lights switched on. One final run-through was called for by the producer, which seemed to go smoothly enough until the cameraman complained that the gold logo reflected the bright lights so much that all the camera could pick up was a white glare. Yet another delay while from somewhere were found a stepladder, a pot of matte varnish, a paintbrush and a man to use all three to tone down the glossy gold. To our amazement, when filming finally started at 11.45pm, it only took two takes: no one forgot their words and the children somehow managed to look fresh and awake. By one in the morning they had each been given a commemorative coin from the bank and a rather expensive toy and had devoured most of the large creamy birthday cake 'prop' from their sketch – a messy affair as the kitchen was closed for the night and hands had to take the place of plates. Sometimes boring, very tiring, but mostly a fascinating experience with fascinating people – a most entertaining way to spend 15 hours.

Chapter Five: Food

If health was always in the minds of the Chinese people, then food was almost more so, which was understandable when you considered how recently near-famine existed in many areas. A common greeting heard frequently was "have you eaten?" which referred not to the timing of your last meal, but whether you had even had one. Even in times of plenty, the preparation of food was still an art form – the earliest known cookbook was said to have been circulated in China about 1,500 years ago. Sadly the typical 'takeaway' food we had sampled at home could never have hoped to reflect the wide variety of cuisine found within the country itself: hot, spicy Sichuan; light flavours of Shandong; slightly sweet, boiled and stewed dishes from Jiangsu, and the better known Guandong (Cantonese) fare. Of all the foods I sampled the most unexpected was the delicious crusty bread from Harbin, in the far north; the most disappointing was the bland boiled mutton of Mongolian hotpot (cooked at the table fondue style); the most aptly named was a dish of crispy rice with sizzling, spitting sauce poured over, called 'Bombs Over Tokyo'.

The Northerners often joked that a dining Cantonese would eat anything with four legs except the table and chairs, and it was from the southern regions that the stories of fresh monkey brains, dog and cat almost certainly came. We once visited a street market in Canton and having passed the fruit, vegetable and souvenir sections we found ourselves in the meat area. Apart from the expected chickens there were cages and baskets containing snakes, cats and some wild animals – all manner of creature could be found for sale. The dogs seemed to be the only animal not sold alive, they were already skinned and hung up much like pigs in an old-fashioned butcher's shop – fortunately they didn't really look like the pets we think of. We were never offered any such exotic foods whilst living in the north, the meat content being pork, chicken or beef, and the one occasion I tried snake I found it rather bitter. In that, we were more fortunate than many visiting delegations who were served 'specialities'. Their stories, plus descriptions of inedible meals, were passed from visitor to prospective visitor, who often brought their own 'emergency' supplies. For some time we benefitted from this, as when they arrived and found things had changed drastically and the food was in fact very good, we were the grateful recipients of such unobtainable luxuries as chocolate bars, cheese slices, Oxo cubes etc.

The Northern cuisine was more akin to our diet than that of the South, containing as it did many flour-based staples such as noodles and steamed bread, as well as the traditional rice. Probably the best known dish of the area was Peking Duck. Our first of many encounters with it was a guests of the Chinese Navy at the 'Sick Duck Restaurant' – so called because of its proximity to the hospital. Waste is a sin in any culture, but one that could never be attributed to this meal as every bit of the duck was used. The meal started with hors d'oeuvres including eggs, cold duck meat, webs (the feet - little flesh, but the idea seemed to be to suck them) and cooked blood set into pâté-like slices. These were all beautifully arranged on serving plates in the design of flowers, birds etc. and garnished with incredible vegetable carvings. (Who else could turn a humble turnip into a blossoming rose?) The second course consisted of hot dishes such as heart and liver, and the third was the duck itself. This was always brought in whole for you to admire and applaud the chef's expertise, and was a deep golden brown and smelled delicious. To achieve a crispy skin without drying out the flesh necessitated forcing air under the skin (often using a bicycle pump) until the duck was completely bloated, basting it well and then filling the body cavity with water and sealing it up. The duck was then roasted in a specially constructed oven, the outside crisping while the flesh steamed from the inside. This method of preparing the famous dish had been used with little change for 600 years. Once the diners had applauded the chef, the bird was returned to the kitchen for slicing (around 120 slices from each duck) and was then served with small, thin pancakes, spring onions and dark bean sauce. With your chopsticks (!) you picked up a pancake and having laid duck, onion and sauce on it, you tucked in the two sides and rolled the whole into a neat parcel resembling a 'spring roll'. Depending on your expertise with chopsticks you could then bite into an absolutely delicious portion of

Peking Duck, or you could lose the lot in a slithering mess onto your plate and bear the ignominy of a waiter presenting you with a fork – fortunately only one's pride suffered: the taste was as good either way! (Prawns and button mushrooms were to be dreaded with chopsticks, the one dropping into its rich red sauce and splashing everyone, the other liable to be squeezed too hard and launched into orbit.) Incidentally the higher up the chopsticks you hold them the more refined and well-bred you are – putting me somewhere below Neanderthal Man. Once everyone was replete, and the guest of honour had been given the duck's tongue, duck soup was served, though seldom did anyone have much room for it. Should you dine at a small restaurant, rather than being the guest at a banquet, you could ask for the carcass of your duck to take home and use as a base for your own soup.

If we at times struggled with chopsticks, so did others struggle with knives and forks. When some Chinese Navy friends were invited on an official visit to the U.K. we asked if there was anything we could do to help them prepare. There followed an evening at our flat serving assorted dishes (including peas!) so they could practise with our cutlery. We heard later that the Chinese Admiral on that visit had had no problem with any of the food served at an official dinner until dessert, part of which was a shortbread biscuit. Unsure of how to pick it up (and having previously been told that to use one's hands was not polite) he speared it forcefully with his fork and nibbled on it. Not wanting him to feel embarrassed the British hosts immediately did likewise.

We attended many banquets both large and small in our years in Beijing and all were equally delicious, although some foods I never really developed a taste for: I'm not sure what part of a shark the 'maw' is, but it always seemed rather tasteless and very chewy, as did the long silvery strands of jellyfish. I shall never forget one particular banquet in the south of China. A particular, and expensive, speciality of the region were sea snails, and a dish of them was ceremoniously placed on the table. I had never fancied the French variety and they at least were often prepared and replaced in the shells, but the ones before me at that dinner were at least four inches long and cooked naturally – head, horns, the lot. The generous hosts offered the delicacy to each of the foreign lady guests in turn, all of whom recoiled in horror, only matched by my horror at the disappointment on the faces of the Chinese hosts: their surprise was turning terribly wrong! With a hint of desperation the hosts held out one of the monsters towards me - "Do you like them?" What could I possibly say but "Yes, I love them." The inevitable happened and I had to chew my way laboriously through six of them – but at least I got to keep the shells as souvenirs! By far the most unpalatable offering to the majority of foreigners, however, was the seaslug, euphemistically referred to as the sea 'cucumber'. Cucumber it certainly wasn't, being a slug-like creature about the size of a courgette and very knobbly. When cooked it was slimy and slightly rubbery and unless you were fortunate enough to be served it sliced up, it was best not looking before putting it into your mouth. Surprisingly I actually developed quite a liking for them, which was "good for my health" as the Chinese loved to say, being helpful in the prevention and treatment of a myriad of ailments from lack of energy to hypersensitivity, arteriosclerosis, hepatitis and lung disorders. Part of this might have been attributable to the tough constitution of the humble slug itself: if broken into several pieces each part would eventually grow into a new slug and it was said that even if disembowelled it could grow complete new inner organs within about seven months! Tomatoes sprinkled with coarse sugar was another dish which at first seemed strange to my taste but for which I developed a great liking, but my all-time favourite turned out to be the so-called Thousand Year Old Eggs. In fact, rather than being particularly old they were merely preserved using an age-old process, and there was a shop to the south of Beijing where you could take your fresh eggs and leave them there to be immersed in their special brine - reputed to be unchanged (only 'topped up') for 100 years. The eggs were ready when the whites had turned into a black, solid jelly and the yolks were black or dark green and still slightly soft.

Banquet food was the 'cordon bleu', but we found the 'everyday' food equally enjoyable. The ayis and other Chinese employees had a canteen nearby the diplomatic compound where they could either eat or fill their food boxes to take away. These rectangular tin boxes were wonderfully versatile, fitting as they did neatly onto the back carrier of a bike, and able to be used in an oven, as a steamer or directly into an open flame to reheat the contents. Many times did Mrs. Yuan and I share each other's lunches, but I think I undoubtedly got the best of the deal - her noodles, fresh vegetables and steamed bread were on a different plane from my boring sandwich, and as for baked beans…!

One dish we sadly never saw outside China was 'jiaozi', tiny 'Cornish pasty' shaped dough parcels filled with chopped pork, vegetables and seasonings and then boiled. Dipped in a mixture of soy sauce, vinegar and ginger they were extremely tasty and incredibly 'more-ish'. In the 7th century they were only eaten by royalty and were sometimes buried as a sacrifice to the dead. On New Year's Day the Emperor was traditionally served a plate of jiaozi, one of which was filled with pieces of silver and placed on top of the others. Should he manage to pick it up with his chopsticks at the first attempt (and they are slippery) it presaged an auspicious year ahead. Fortunately these delicacies later became available to everyone. A similar type of meat 'parcel', a 'baozi' was shaped more like a dumpling and steamed rather than boiled, giving it an entirely different taste. The most famous restaurant for baozi was in Tianjin, a seaport to the south east of the capital, which served an amazing variety of them and had the intriguing name of 'Goubuli'. The literal translation of this was 'No Dog Inside' and it was a much argued point as to whether it meant there was no dog meat in the baozi or that you would be of no more account than a dog had you never partaken of the wonderful fare the restaurant had to offer.

Just as there was a vast range from banquet to everyday food, so too was there (by the late 80s) a great choice of dining venues, ranging from 'luxury' to 'eat-on-the-streets'. (The first public restaurants began to appear in China as early as 770 BC). Most popular amongst the expat. community were the many 'joint venture' hotels in whose restaurants you could dine as well as anywhere in the world, and as the variety of nationalities within the city grew, so too did the range of food offered.

Pizza restaurants, fish and chip nights, and one establishment (opened by the Air Catering Company from the airport) were so determined not to lose anyone's custom that they featured a different country's cuisine every night: Monday – England, Tuesday – Hungary, Wednesday – Italy, Thursday – Russia, Friday – France, Saturday – Japan and Sunday – India. Should you wish a less formal venue you could head to the south of Tian An Men Square and enter the portals of Kentucky Fried Chicken where, apart from the queues of local people, you could be in London: the food, the clean toilets – the only difference being that the locally produced potatoes didn't make good chips so mashed potatoes were served instead. It was a sad reflection on the power of influence from the West that young Chinese people would queue for hours and spend vast sums of money on food far inferior to their own simply because it came from abroad. Just as we were leaving Beijing in 1990 the unmistakable roof of Pizza Hut appeared and rumours were rife that McDonalds was not far behind. According to local gossip, they had been set to open some time before and had even gone so far as to raise its own beef and plant its own potatoes when the question of 'spot checks' on restaurants raised its ugly head. Word was that the Chinese management refused to accept unannounced inspections, so the opening was cancelled. Such sophistication in hotels and restaurants had been hard to achieve at first, being a completely 'foreign' concept to the Chinese. Staff were surprised that they had to really 'serve' the customers and couldn't sweep up round them and turn out the lights at 9.30 pm, so lengthy training sessions were essential. On one occasion a foreign guest had dared to point out to a waitress that there was a large chip in his glass: without hesitation she picked up the glass, turned it around and told him to drink from the other side. When an hotel felt themselves ready to accept guests they would announce their 'soft opening': rooms would be offered at reduced rates on the understanding that the staff and whole system were still very new and teething troubles were par to the course. After a month or two, if all went well (or maybe even if it didn't!) the 'hard opening' followed and the hotel was fully operational. Joint ventures had great advantages over wholly Chinese owned establishments, as their management and many staff benefitted from years of experience overseas, but even they had their moments – it was rumoured that when the first of these many joint hotels opened they discovered that their contract allowed them to accept guests but not to import food. The prospect of trying to operate on the local supplies, especially of meat, forced them into an immediate signing of, and paying for, another contract. It was amazing how quickly you grew accustomed to the choice and quality of food, and easy to forget the diet of cabbage, the awe on the Chinese faces gazing through windows at the palatial foyers and restaurants into which they were barred entry (except, for some reason, in the south of China where they were permitted to stand around in the hotels, taking photos of each other). I remember the moment when I first dined after many years in a truly Western restaurant and was so overcome by the sight of green vegetables that I even ate the decorative parsley off the plates. Years of deprivation did make you a lot more conscious of the appalling waste we took for granted, even if it did once lead me to drinking the bowl of tea I was served not realising it was meant as a fingerbowl.

Remarkable changes took place not only on the 'western front' but in Chinese restaurants geared to the entertainment of foreigners and their Chinese hosts. The white dagoba in Beihai Park, especially seen at night, must have been one of the most atmospheric venues for a restaurant and one where you could almost feel the history in the very fabric of the walls. The dishes served all dated from the original recipes from the kitchens of the Qing Dynasty, although bears' paws, sharks' fins and venison no longer featured - no expense had been spared for the Imperial Court. Certain items might have been omitted, but the artistry of presentation remained as superb as ever - a kind of 'mock turtle' soup was often served with what appeared to be tiny turtles floating on the surface, but they were in fact meticulously sculpted mushrooms; the cold meats were arranged in the shape of the Imperial dragon and phoenix; even the yellow tableware was an exact copy of that used in the Court. Had we been dining with the Emperor or the Empress Dowager there would have been literally hundreds of different dishes, many of which would have been barely sampled and many even left untouched - as for us, whenever I dined there I ate every bit! Even breakfast would have seen up to forty dishes offered, and should the Emperor have gone away on a tour of inspection or to one of the country palaces, fifty or sixty cooks would be amongst the entourage, plus the eunuch food tasters. It was on such trips that he could enjoy a more relaxed atmosphere and eat with accompanying members of the family: in the capital, except for official banquets, he always dined alone. One of the Empress Dowager Cixi's favourite dishes was small sesame seed buns which you partially opened rather in the fashion of pitta bread and then stuffed with minced beef. (It does sound remarkably akin to our modern-day beefburger, but they do say nothing is new!) The other speciality served only at this particular restaurant were miniature corn cakes shaped like hollow, slightly rounded pyramids, about the size of a thimble. Corn cakes used to be enjoyed by the commoners of Beijing and only came to be a part of the Imperial diet after 1900. It was in that year that the foreign powers occupied the capital, forcing Cixi to make a hurried and ignominious departure for Xi'an. To avoid detection she rode not in her customary sedan chair but in a humble cart, and her entourage disguised her as a peasant. During the long journey she became very hungry and resorted to trying one of the corn cakes the poor, and genuine, peasants had to survive on. To everyone's surprise she found it delicious (she must have been hungry - I've tried one!), and on her eventual return to 'her' capital she instructed the chefs to prepare corn cakes for her. Ever mindful of their reputations, not to mention their lives, the chefs realised that her extreme hunger had fooled her palate and that they dared not serve up the genuine article, which she would undoubtedly have found decidedly unpleasant. Ever resourceful, they made their own version using fine sugar, cornflour and chestnuts instead of coarse corn. It appeared she never realised the deception.

Another restaurant with Imperial connections was a totally unique venture started by the daughter of one of the Court chefs, Madame Lili, who opened up two very small, adjoining one-storey houses into a 'restaurant', but one so small that it held only one table, with an absolute maximum of twelve guests, and a hat stand. The adjoining house served primarily as the kitchen and, presumably, the living quarters for the family themselves. As somewhere to dine with good, freshly cooked food and a feeling of intimacy that was the place, although you never really felt you were truly in someone's home, as it was all too sterile and appeared unlived-in. Of course there were sceptics, and I often heard jokes about there probably being a dishwasher, freezer and microwave hidden in yet another house: certainly there were no signs of any dirty dishes when you were invited to view the tiny kitchen after you had eaten.

I was extremely fortunate that on two separate occasions I did dine in a 'genuine' Chinese home. The first was during the celebrations for the Spring Festival and we were invited to join friends who lived in the country. There we must have eaten the freshest food ever - all (pork, chicken, eggs, fruit and vegetables) were produced in the village, and when I complimented the hostess on one particular vegetable dish she immediately went outside to pick more to cook for me. The rice in particular I shall always remember, having a nutty flavour I have never come across before or since. The second 'home-cooked' lunch was on a trip that Mrs. Yuan and I took to Shanhaiguan, where the Great Wall disappears into the sea on the east coast of China. Spurning the restaurant designed for the foreign tourists, she led me off down a side street where she had seen a small, roughly written sign saying simply 'noodles'. At the door we were met by the owner/cook; a small lady of great age and enormous energy and personality, who ushered us into her tiny one-room house. We were invited to sit on bench seats by a large wooden table which took up most of the room. The only other furniture was a large sideboard, the top of which was covered in family photos, and, under the one window and built into the alcove was the *kang* or family bed. The kang was the traditional type of bed found in all homes in China and ranged from extremely ornate carved wood affairs with silk drapery and cushions, to the basic design we saw here made of concrete and wood. Designed for use by the entire family they were built high enough off the ground for a charcoal brazier to be placed underneath in the winter to provide heat for the occupants. While I looked around fascinated at this insight into a Chinese home, our hostess went into the narrow passageway leading from the doorway to a tiny courtyard in the rear where she prepared our lunch. The 'cooker' was a concrete platform with an open fire underneath and with two holes in the platform itself of exactly the right size to fit wok or saucepan. All the noodles the lady served she had made herself, as were the many sauces offered to us, ranging from slightly sweet to very spicy. I for one grossly overate, as the noodles and sauce were the best I could ever imagine eating, but we finally managed to tear ourselves away. I didn't know who enjoyed the experience most, myself or our hostess - I was the first foreigner who had ever eaten in her tiny 'restaurant'/home.

When we had first arrived in China, and food was hard to come by, fellow Attachés were more than satisfied with any meal you could offer, but as Western restaurants and supermarkets mushroomed they expected a far higher class of fare and one which we found became rather repetitive. Dinners ceased to be a challenge or an adventure, and it was for that reason that we searched for something 'different' and discovered the newly opened 'Genghis Khan' restaurant. In a field to the east of the city centre, it was a group of yurts, or circular Mongolian tents, made from basic wooden frames covered with animal skins and supported by thick tree trunks painted red and gold. Inside, the guests sat on stools around circular tables - it was quite bare except for a few pot plants. The first time we dined at the Genghis Khan, together with our twenty or so invited guests, was in November, which was a great mistake as the yurts were unheated! Fortunately they all entered into the spirit of the evening, even if they had to dine with their coats on. The food served to us was typically Mongolian and was somewhat similar to Chinese with the exception of toffied camel hump ('different', but I wouldn't mind if I never ate it again). The most delicious dish of the evening was succulent leg of lamb, served whole with a lethal-looking Mongolian knife sticking out of it with which you served yourself slices of meat. Rounding off the meal with cups of tea made with fermented mare's milk, we were invited to step outside to watch the entertainment: bare-chested, muscled Mongolian wrestlers. Having displayed their athletic skills we were asked if any one of us wished to 'have a go'. I suspected that to be a rhetorical question but the Japanese Attaché, a tiny man but presumably versed in the martial arts, couldn't wait. What could have developed into an extremely difficult situation ensued, as both men were by nature very unwilling to lose face and were filled with national pride. The Mongolian certainly had the edge in sheer bulk, but was obviously in a dilemma as to whether to toe the party line on respecting foreigners and 'throw' the contest. To our great relief and eternal gratitude the Polish Attaché (no small man himself) saved the day by firmly separating the two wrestling figures and holding up an arm of each. "We have two winners" he announced, "let us toast them both", and led them back into the yurt for more wine and tea. A true diplomat.

Unless you could speak and read Chinese pretty well perfectly, you were inclined to gravitate to restaurants which were geared to foreigners, although the 'masses' restaurants did look so much more fun. Just once I did eat in one such place, but it was by accident – albeit a very lucky one. For some time I had heard people talk of the wonderful Russian restaurant close to the zoo, so planned to take my mother there during her holiday in China. Just by the entrance to the zoo itself we saw a Russian style building, but it appeared very closed, and there were so many similar buildings in the immediate area that the restaurant could have been any one of them. Thinking that it must have been accessible from inside the zoo itself we went in and walked along close to the outer wall until we came across a rather unprepossessing place but from which emanated the most delicious smell - we must have found it. A waitress showed us to a table and indicated a counter on which were displayed plates of food from which we were invited to make our choice. Knowing nothing about Russian food and unable to understand the names of the dishes (in much the same way as 'shepherd's pie' or 'cottage pie' or 'toad in the hole' gives you no idea as to the ingredients) we asked her to make a selection for us. While she was sorting that out I went to another counter to buy a plastic jug of beer and two glasses. Looking around the room, which was packed, it bore more of a resemblance to a works canteen than a top class restaurant; plastic cloths on the tables still bore the remains of the previous diners' meals and on the floor were fish and chicken bones dropped there by the diners or swept off the tables by waitresses between customers. These remains were cleaned up every night, but there was no way it could be achieved during the day as the restaurant was working flat out just keeping up with the number of people waiting to eat - and they certainly didn't seem to mind the crunchiness underfoot. It was obviously a very popular place - no wonder everyone kept recommending it to me. Our meal, however, showed no sign of any Russian influence: it was delicious but quite definitely Chinese, as were all the meals we could see being consumed with great gusto around us. It became increasingly obvious that we were in the wrong place - and therefore no wonder that we were the only foreigners there: it was the restaurant for Chinese visitors to the zoo! We had been made very welcome and the food was not only very good but the portions were extremely large, so much so that there was no way we could hope to eat it all. Having paid the very cheap bill, on the way out we noticed our waitress call to two rather urchin-looking boys in clean but threadbare clothes who were sitting outside. As soon as we were actually off the premises they were seated at our table and in record time had virtually scraped the serving plates clean. What a refreshing change to the way we wasted so much. We had missed out on genuine Russian food, but had had the unique experience of eating where absolutely nothing was geared to the foreigner.

Over time, more and more individuals opened tiny crowded restaurants, all trying to outdo each other. All were full to capacity, but it was noticed that one in particular was so popular that queues stretched along the nearby street. Then suddenly one day it was gone: their popularity had allegedly been discovered to be attributed to the minute amount of heroin added to each dish to leave diners desperate for more!

In almost every guide book you are strongly advised to eat nothing bought 'on the streets', but in all my time in Beijing the only food that upset me was a beefburger from a Western hotel. One of the reasons for this might well have been the incredibly high temperatures at which the food was cooked - flames literally leaped several feet high from an expertly managed wok. One of the most exciting places to eat al fresco was 'food alley'; rows of stalls set up along the pavement on a stretch of Chang An. All manner of meals and snacks were offered and each stall holder vied with the rest for your custom. Kebabs were a great favourite, served on skewers or, in some cases, on spokes from a bicycle wheel. By far the biggest crowd-puller as far as the foreigners were concerned was the amazing noodle maker: starting with a lump of dough, he manipulated it with incredible speed and dexterity until he had pulled it out between his hands into strings of noodles resembling a skein of wool. Faster and faster he moved, and thinner and thinner the noodles grew, until he considered them ready to boil. Heaven forbid that such amazing talent should ever die out with the increasing desire for mechanisation. Less permanent were the itinerant food sellers, but if you headed away from the tourist routes you would usually manage to find them. In the winter months my particular favourites were steamed sweet potatoes (warming for both hands and stomach), and large pancakes covered on one side with egg and then rolled around a twist of fried dough liberally smeared with spicy sauce. In the summer these delicacies were replaced by ice lollies, ranging from rather watery 'fruit' varieties, to disgusting lumpy ones made with sweet beans, to lovely milky ones. The selling of these ice lollies was almost totally the domain of elderly grandmothers, intentionally meant to give them a nice little income, get them out of their homes into the sunny weather, and provide an opportunity to meet people. Very early every morning they would make their way to the depot to collect their wooden carts of lollies which they would then wheel off to their 'pitch'. There being no refrigeration it was essential to keep the carts as cold as possible, which they achieved by covering them in extremely thick cotton 'duvets'. To avoid opening the door on the top too often, a selection of 'ready use' lollies were kept in wide-mouthed vacuum flasks with cork stoppers. Towards the end of our time in Beijing, a Chinese ice-cream parlour opened offering all manner of flavours at a very cheap price, but I suspect (and hope) the lolly ladies will go on forever despite any competition. Another popular hot weather snack was sliced watermelon, being full of refreshing juice - and very messy to eat. By each vendor's stall was a square wooden box with a mesh grille over the top: as you ate a mouthful of the melon you spat the pips into the box, and then threw the rind in when you'd finished. The design was such that the pips fell through into the bottom section and the rinds stayed on top.   I wasn't sure what they were used for, but learned that thrifty housewives salted the rinds and served them sprinkled with sesame oil. The seeds they cleaned, dried in the sun and stir-fried.

Almost all the food I tasted in China I enjoyed and have not tasted the like since. Food to the Chinese people was more than just a necessary part of life - it was to be savoured and to be visually pleasing as well. Many foods were also symbolic, such as the humble peach (more pear-shaped than ours): the Goddess Wangmu was reputed to have a magic peach tree which took 3,000 years to blossom and another 3,000 to bear fruit, so thereafter peaches were considered to be symbolic of long life (if not patience!).

Chapter Six: Health and Medicine

Paranoia was probably the best word to describe the Chinese attitude to ill-health; they were terrified of being taken ill, probably with good reason as medical services left a lot to be desired and treatment could be expensive. This was most likely why so many of the population continued to wear thick, thermal-type underwear long after we would have discarded them. These were very often visible under rolled up trouser legs should it get a little too hot: the most colourful seemed to belong to the Army (who wore uniform both on and off duty) who favoured a sort of cerise/fuchsia mixture. When Anna, as a young child, developed a sudden high temperature on a train, the attendants insisted on turning off the air-conditioning (in August) for fear of her getting chilled. Mrs. Yuan was all for taking her to the nearest hospital for an injection, but I was more concerned that our fellow passengers and ourselves would suffer severe heat-stroke.

There were many ways in which you could help to ensure continued good health: eating certain foods (asparagus as a preventative against cancer for instance) and keeping your natural body force, or 'qi', flowing in the correct balance. This entailed a series of qigong or taiqiquan exercises performed every day, preferably next to a pine tree as they give off more oxygen than other trees. (Perhaps that's why the Highlands of Scotland boast such beautiful air). Nor was the attention to health and fitness entirely a personal one: as early as 1951 the government had produced a series of exercises for adults, followed after a few years by similar ones for children, and in 1954 they decreed that every work unit should have ten minutes of compulsory exercises twice a day. Well after thirty years on, and in schools, offices and factories everything still stopped at 10am and 4pm while students and workers congregated in communal areas and began a set series of exercises to special music broadcast on the radio. Young children also spent some time every day performing eye exercises consisting of movement and massage, designed to preserve good sight well into old age. At the other end of the scale, the elderly were not forgotten: apart from personal regimes of qigong etc.

ballroom dancing was suddenly promoted as an ideal form of exercise for the older generation, being both gentle and sociable, and many a group could be seen both in parks and residential areas.

In the past it was also your doctor's responsibility to keep you fit, a task he took seriously as you paid him a fee all the while you were well, but stopped payment should you fall ill as he was deemed to have failed you. Mrs. Yuan's father was an expert herbalist and had a natural diagnostic gift – he could tell what was wrong with a person, even a total stranger, just by looking at his or her face. He didn't even need to talk to the person before not only confirming any illness they had, but also spotting any others present but undetected at the time. Doctors in the past could also make surprisingly accurate diagnoses just by feeling the pulses in both wrists: any irregularity in speed, volume of blood etc. and contrasts between the two pulses could pinpoint problems. This form of diagnosis was essential in dealing with women as the doctor wasn't allowed to examine a female patient or touch any part of her body except the wrists, and she certainly wouldn't have answered personal questions either. The most she would have done was to point at a model to indicate where she felt pain.

Should you, despite all precautions, fall ill then a variety of treatments were available, ranging from herbal medicines to acupuncture to moxibustion and, in later times, Western medicines too. A visit to a herbal pharmacy was an experience in itself: walls lined floor to ceiling with drawers containing all manner of herbs and dried parts of animals which would be meticulously weighed and mixed according to the doctor's prescription. Some mixtures had to be handled with extreme care as boiling for 5 minutes released healing properties, but if allowed to boil for longer potentially lethal toxins were released. For the more cautious it was possible to buy ready-prepared herbal remedies and one particularly effective one which I used (it resembled deer droppings and undoubtedly tasted worse) could cure the common cold overnight, especially if taken in conjunction with a bowl of hot noodles with very hot chilli sauce. The Chinese cold virus unfortunately proved to be a different strain than the British one, and my supplies of herbal remedies were of no use when taken home.

A lot of the theory behind cures in China was based on the 'qi' and the fact that imbalance caused illness. Fighting the illness itself was of lesser importance than getting the 'qi' back into balance, for once that was achieved the body could fight for itself. For that reason two people with totally differing ailments could be given the same medicine, as the prescription was based on the type of 'qi' imbalance and not on the type of illness.

Hospitalisation of serious cases was to us like being time-warped back to Florence Nightingale and the war hospitals: the doctors were mostly very proficient and highly trained but the equipment was old, if not antiquated, and hygiene and sterilisation left a great deal to be desired. One visiting foreign doctor once commented that the high success rate they seemed to achieve in post-operative care was due less to the conditions than to the massive amounts of antibiotics prescribed – enough to kill just about every infection, if not the patient as well. For that reason we always carried sterile hypodermic needles with us in case of accident. There was another, more positive side, to the hospitals and one which we only came to hear about through a tragic death. An outbreak of encephalitis, which had spread through China, reached Beijing, causing quite a few deaths amongst the Chinese population. We were all vaccinated, but not so fortunate was a foreign student in his twenties who contracted the disease. His parents were contacted immediately and offers made of either a flight home or the bringing to China of a specialist from the student's own country. Both were declined. His parents considered that the treatment he was receiving in Beijing was equal to that which he would receive anywhere else, but with one added 'feature' – the nursing care. What was lacking in surroundings and equipment was more than compensated for by the high degree of good old-fashioned 'loving care'. Nothing was too much trouble and the nurses quite literally 'willed' their patients to fight for life. What an amazing contrast that was to the 'take it or leave it' attitude we had encountered in so many places and situations, the direst consequence of which was reported to have befallen a young visitor to Tibet. Arriving by plane, he had suffered severe altitude sickness and, realising that medical help was needed, his friends rushed him to the hotel and sat him in a chair whilst they summoned assistance. The girl manning the crowded reception desk was loath to serve anyone and certainly wasn't going to be interrupted in her slow dealings with the queue of tourists booking in. By the time she could be persuaded to deal with them the young man had died.

When we first arrived in Beijing many medical, and all dental, problems necessitated a trip to Hong Kong, but later improvements in standards, and easing of restrictions on Chinese nationals studying or training abroad, allowed us access to expert local practitioners. I shall never forget my first encounter with the reception area of the dental hospital: none of the colourful posters encouraging children to brush their teeth; we were met instead by glass-fronted display cases full of horribly decayed teeth displayed next to gleaming white, smiling, dentures.

Despite the almost hypochondriac tendencies of the older Chinese people I met, many of them were surprisingly ignorant of some facts which I had always considered to be common knowledge. When Mrs. Yuan's daughter was due to have her baby some amazing traditions emerged: for the first few days it was considered harmful for the baby to suckle from the mother, as the colostrum was thought to be unsuitable. During that time the poor mother was fed copious quantities of eggs and brown sugar and was allowed no visitors outside of the immediate family for fourteen days. I don't know if German Measles is found in China, but she certainly had never heard of it and of its potentially disastrous effect on the foetus. Possibly the most alarming omission in her medical knowledge was that it is the father and not the mother who determines the sex of the child – to think that awareness of that fact could have freed so many women of the guilt and stigma of failure to produce a son.

Chapter Seven: Transport

A game of virtual reality where you are walking through a gloomy room, muscles tensed, waiting for your 'enemy' to jump out at you has a marked resemblance to driving in China in the early days of our time there. Street lighting consisted of thin electric wires stretched across the street some distance apart, with one 40 watt bulb – complete with shade! – hanging from the centre of each wire. The myriad bicycles and carts were all black and the riders and drivers dressed in dark colours, and to further ensure their near invisibility to car drivers their conveyances had neither lights nor reflectors. Car headlights also failed to improve visibility as it was illegal to use anything more than sidelights in case you dazzled oncoming cyclists. At around 10.30 pm the traffic had usually decreased to a mere trickle so all traffic lights were switched to flashing amber, not that their use made an awful lot of difference to many road users. Cyclists and farm cart drivers in particular seemed to be oblivious to all other traffic, 'rules of the road' or danger and assumed you had telepathic powers to predict when they would turn across in front of you. I suppose if you had always driven or ridden along a certain track and someone then turned it into a road and put cars on it, you might well have assumed right of way on the grounds that you were there first. Fortunately cars were in the minority (there being no privately owned ones for the Chinese) or there would certainly have been many more serious accidents.

As diplomats we were allowed to drive our own car (other foreign residents had to employ drivers), but we first had to obtain Chinese diplomatic licences. We were fortunate to hold British licences which we could simply exchange, otherwise we would have had to take a Chinese driving test which was pretty intense and included manoeuvring slalom-fashion between rows of poles and reversing into confined spaces. In order to swop our licences we first had to have a medical examination at the foreigners' section of the Capital Hospital. Only the fittest were to drive and we were tested for everything possible from high blood pressure to abnormalities of heart, lungs, liver and spleen. The sight test chart was sensibly designed both for those who could not understand

Chinese characters ('us') and those who could not read the alphabet ('them'). It was also ideal for small children who would not comprehend either of the two. It consisted of rows of capital letter Es, either facing forwards or backwards or rotated to face up in the air or down to the ground. You covered one eye with a long-handled wooden spoon and with the other simply pointed in the direction in which the E was facing. We reached one major snag when it came to the colour-blindness test as, although he can tell red from green, Mike did have problems with some of the other colours, and couldn't pick out the pig or cow shapes from amongst the coloured dots. The examining doctors were far from happy, but the Embassy nurse who had accompanied us knew them well and also had a great sense of humour. She persuaded them that he could tell if a traffic light was red, and that if he ever saw a REAL pig or cow in the road he would not only recognise it for what it was but would certainly either drive round it or stop the car. They too saw the funny side, and we got our licences.

Our first sortie was to the petrol station, of which there were only two in Beijing where foreigners were allowed to buy fuel, both situated near the diplomatic housing areas. As we were restricted as to how far we could drive, there was no need for additional pumps for our use further afield, although it was essential to set off with a reasonable full tank, as no other petrol stations were allowed to serve us. Petrol was very cheap, and even discounted to us if we used coupons purchased from the Embassy. A 'Health and Safety' inspector would probably have suffered from apoplexy had he witnessed the manner of filling the tank: the attendant leant against the car with a lit cigarette dangling from his mouth, his only concession to the displayed safety notice enjoining customers to refrain from smoking was to turn his head slightly away. We silently prayed that the wind wouldn't blow hot ash in the wrong direction.

We soon learned some of the driving techniques unique to this country. In order to drive across a lane of traffic it wasn't just a case of waiting for a break in the stream of cars – that was the easy part – you had first to cross a much more undisciplined stream of bicycles. If you waited for a break in them you might be static for weeks, so you had to very slowly inch forward with bikes whizzing by inches from your front bumper until suddenly one swerved behind you rather than in front, and as if by magic all the others followed his lead and you were through. You then only had the cars to contend with, except of course the exception to every rule, such as the old man we saw pedalling slowly and obliviously the wrong way down the fast lane of a very busy road. Intersections were controlled either by lights or by policemen standing on podia and giving rather vague hand-signals and unintelligible verbal instructions over a loudspeaker. There is a story that during the Cultural Revolution when red was the colour of the moment, traffic signals were altered so that red meant 'go' and green meant 'stop'. It was said to have made no difference at all to the driving or accident rate. Although we didn't have to take a test, we did buy a copy of the Highway Code to study – most of it was rather similar to our own but there were much more rigorous restrictions on the driver himself. Whilst in control of a vehicle it was illegal to eat, drink, smoke, talk or sleep – this latter for, although largely ignored by, the many mule cart drivers who climbed up on top of their loads and left their mules to tread their weary but well recognised paths home. We had occasion one dark night to happen across a black cart pulled by a black mule – he did know his way home, but his sleeping driver had failed to instruct him in the art of staying to one side of the road rather than wandering down the middle. It was also illegal to move anything at the site of an accident until the police gave permission – even if it meant driving over glass bottles smashed in their fall from an overturned truck, or circumnavigating a dead body. One Chinese traffic law I felt could well have been emulated by many of the Western countries was the lack of any 'safe' alcohol limit – if you had drunk ANY alcohol at all and were involved in an accident you were automatically seen to be at fault.

The few cars that were around were mostly taxis: large, old-fashioned saloons called Shanghais, which bore a resemblance to a 1950s Mercedes. Occasionally you might have caught a glimpse of the 'official' car used by high-ranking cadres, a '*Hongqi*' or 'Red Flag' – a veritable Rolls Royce of a car. Not only could we drive ourselves, we were also able to have a car shipped out from the U.K. The Foreign Office stressed that all British Embassy cars, both private and official, should be British, but after an embarrassing episode when nearly all official cars were off the road for some time awaiting spare parts, the policy was relaxed and Toyotas purchased. The one stalwart exception to this was the Ambassador's superb Daimler.

Prior to our first stay we had had no time to organise a car so had been permitted to buy locally, but only from other foreigners, and were fortunate to find a Toyota Landcruiser being sold by the United Nations. In 1986 we imported a new Range Rover. This had originally been part of an order for a Middle Eastern customer but for some reason (coup, assassination etc?) had never been collected. We must have had one of the few cars in China with automatic transmission, air conditioning and an armoured fuel tank. As it was necessary for us to collect the car from the docks at Tianjin we had booked an Embassy minibus and driver to leave early in the morning to avoid lunchtime closures. Spare seats in the bus were filled with the two drivers' friends, wives, girlfriends etc. with one reserved for another Brit. whose car was also ready for collection. Having waited at the Embassy for him for over half an hour, we drove to his flat, his girlfriend's flat, and any other place we thought he might have spent the night – but failed to get a reply at any of them. Arranging for one of the drivers to drive the car back, we admitted defeat and left without him, by which time we were very late. Fortunately the Chinese staff had done this many times before, so upon arrival at Tianjin they set-to with the enormous amount of paperwork – plus a few packets of Western cigarettes that we'd been advised to take along. It all seemed to be going smoothly – too smoothly – when it was suddenly declared to be lunch time: down pens, lock doors and off to the canteen, leaving us at a total loss as to know what to do. Not so our drivers. The Seamen's Club served a delicious lunch, after which we all sat in the minibus until 'siesta' time was over. More papers, more cigarettes and suddenly we were told that we could take the cars away, and were issued with the numbers of the crates which housed them. Following directions to the dockside itself we were met by row upon long row of crates stacked two or three high and resembling a modern-day Great Wall: all were numbered but were not stacked in any numerical sequence whatsoever. The crane driver was standing by, but pointed out that he only moved things – he had no idea where ours might be: there was only one answer; splitting up, we took a couple of rows each until someone spotted them. Even when the crates were finally deposited at our feet, we were expected to break them open ourselves. To our delight, and surprise, both cars started comparatively easily, and with a final dispensing of pieces of paper and the last of the cigarettes we were on our way home – or so we thought. Despite the fact that we were hours later than planned and that it was almost dark, a promise had obviously been made to the young ladies accompanying us of a visit to Tianjin's famous food street. It was actually a two-storey open-plan building in the shape of a cross, housing nothing but restaurants, food shops and fast-food stalls – except that by the time we arrived there most of the stalls had packed up and all the shops were shut. Fortunately they thought the restaurant prices too high to tempt them to stay for dinner, as Mike for one couldn't have eaten a thing, having found driving a totally unfamiliar car, in the dark, down narrow lanes full of meandering pedestrians, in an unknown city, a far from relaxing pastime and certainly not one to stimulate the appetite. We arrived home late and tired, having had a surprisingly uneventful journey except for once losing sight of the minibus ahead and once doing an unintentional emergency stop when Mike tried to put his foot down on the clutch only to discover that in an automatic car that's where the brake was!

Getting the car was one thing, but to be able to actually use it on the roads of China necessitated applying for Chinese licence plates. Diplomatic plates at that time bore two sets of numbers and the character for 'diplomat'. The first number denoted the Embassy (United Kingdom was 223) and the second indicated the position within that Embassy of the owner of the car. An Ambassador was always 0001, a Naval Attaché usually 0007. This system could cause great confusion in cases of accidents or traffic infringements – witnesses often only remembered the second of the two sets of numbers and you were likely to get the blame for the sins of your opposite number at some Embassy you might hardly have heard of.

Thinking that we'd dealt with all the vehicular red tape, we were then told that there was yet one more hurdle: the road test and engine inspection. For that the engine had to be pristine, as clean as new, for the traffic police did not want to poke around amongst a whole lot of oil and grime. We dutifully hosed it all out and took it to the inspection point where all went well until one of the police took it for a spin around the block to test steering and brakes – both of which were power assisted. Whether a Range Rover reacted faster than he was used to, or whether he was confused by the automatic transmission but he came within inches of demolishing several market stalls and a few bystanders before screeching to a halt and announcing that the car had passed the test.

Our euphoria at having not only our own car, but such a prestigious one at that, was rather short-lived when it developed a most unnerving habit of stalling unexpectedly and refusing to start again. Several Embassy wives had organised a tour to a jade factory and I went along as one of the drivers and providers of transport. Passengers embarked, we set off in loose convoy just at the tail end of the morning rush hour. As we approached a very busy crossroads near the Temple of Heaven the traffic lights changed leaving me one side while all the others drove on – which I would dearly have loved to have done too when they changed again, but the car had stalled and resolutely refused to start. Emergency flashers and hand signals seemed to do little to appease the ever increasing number of angry drivers to my rear and in no time at all the crossroads were a chaotic melee. After what seemed an eternity a traffic policeman left his roadside 'box' and came over – to sort it all out I naively believed. His stern "You can't park here" left me temporarily speechless. I explained that far from being parked, my car had in fact completely broken down – "then mend it" was the reply. The whole dialogue seemed to be fast disintegrating into a Chinese version of "There's a hole in my bucket". Finally, begrudgingly accepting that I really didn't have any idea as to the fault, or how to rectify it, he told me to move the wretched car into the bike track and out of the way. By that time one of my passengers was all for telling him exactly where to go, but I had decided to use more devious means: loudly enough for the inevitable crowd of onlookers to hear I apologised profusely for breaking down on his crossroads, guaranteed that I would never take that particular road again and sympathised with his misfortune that I should have come along to ruin his entire day. Of course I would gladly move the offending vehicle but, pathetic creatures that we were, three women just weren't strong enough to shift anything that size. There could have been no doubt that he realised all was being spoken very 'tongue-in-cheek' but he didn't dare lose face by refusing assistance to this grovelling foreigner in front of such a large, and ever growing, crowd. As the three of us began to try to push he was forced into helping, but he had his pride and only exerted just enough pressure to start us off, and then only using thumb and two fingers of one hand. It could only have been termed a 'technical push', but neither of us had lost face and we parted as equals. There still remained the problem of getting started, so I headed off in the direction of a 'telephone' sign hung up outside a grey-looking block of flats. The phone seemed about as reliable as the Range Rover, but finally help was summoned and the Defence Section driver, Lao Li, was on his way. By that time I feared the passengers might be getting a little fed up, so pointed out all the good points about our situation: on one corner was an old man selling cold drinks, on another a granny with her ice lollies, and right by us the public toilet. My enthusiastic tour was cut short by the arrival of the sewage collection truck, which proceeded very noisily to pump out the holding tanks next to us. The smell was overpowering, but at that point, rather like the cavalry in any good John Wayne film, the other cars of our party appeared with the offer of lifts. One wife gratefully accepted but the other, quite newly arrived in China, said she'd not had such an opportunity of seeing life on the streets and didn't intend to miss a minute of it.

Mike and Lao Li arrived and set to to find the fault. It almost certainly derived from the fuel pump so Lao Li lay down under the car and gave it a few good blows with a piece of wood. Two elderly Chinese men walked past and, on seeing the inert legs sticking out just behind the front wheels, one of them declared in a very resigned voice "the foreigners have killed another one."

Our problems were finally solved with the help of a wonderful Israeli mechanic, married to an Austrian diplomat. He suspected that whilst standing around at a dealer's in the U.K. the car had been used as a quick source of spare parts, and upon our buying it an old starter motor and fuel pump had been installed. Not only infuriating, but extremely costly as we had to pay to have the necessary replacements flown out to us.

After months of frustration and distrust of the car, it was finally reliable once more and it was with pride that we drove up to the front doors of The Great Hall of The People to attend a reception: after all, we were in the make of car favoured by Royalty. 'Pride comes before...' etc. The policeman in charge of marshalling cars and guests took one look at our vehicle and directed us to the bus park! Size was the deciding factor, not class!

Should you import a car into China but not take it out again you were liable to pay an enormous sum in tax (often far more than the actual value of the car itself). That effectively deterred foreigners from selling them off for profit to anyone except another diplomat, or from starting up a black market. An Australian Attaché had the misfortune to fall foul of this law through no fault of his own: shortly before he was due to leave China he advertised his car for sale within the diplomatic community and had several people show an interest. One particular African gentleman asked to test-drive it first and, seeing no reason to refuse such a request, was given the keys. That was the last the Australian ever saw of him, or his car. The African diplomat's Ambassador washed his hands of the whole thing: there was obviously a black market operating somewhere, and if the car was never recovered the poor Australian would be liable to pay the hefty tax. (We ourselves left before the matter was settled).

An amazing increase in the volume of traffic must have been one of the greatest shocks upon our return after three years, together with continuing building and improving of the road network. The road to the airport was no longer a narrow track but had been widened and resurfaced and there were great flyovers at the intersections, with bright arc lights. Almost all the major roads had brighter, more effective lighting and we were allowed to use headlights, although only dipped. Driving conditions might have been easier, but the 'down' side was that we could no longer use our balconies on warm evenings, not because of pollution but because it proved impossible to hold a conversation above the roar of the traffic below. Gone were the teenagers skateboarding every evening down the ring road itself, kites flying behind them in the breeze. It was busy 24 hours a day – and to think that when we had watched it being built we really believed the motorway-sized roads were over-ambitious and would forever be underused! To alleviate the impending traffic jams it was rumoured that restrictions would be introduced allowing only odd numbered licence plates access to the city on certain days, and even numbered ones on others. I seemed to remember hearing that such a system had worked well in other countries, but I had serious doubts as regards the average Chinese driver, especially ones coming in from outside. As no vehicle was privately owned, but would have been the property of a commune or work unit, there would be little chance of a driver knowing or remembering the licence plate – and just supposing one ended in a nought!

Not only were there many more cars, there were many more models: the Japanese seemed to have cornered the market in importing vehicles, but there were also more modern Chinese ones too and even a joint venture company, with America, producing a Beijing Jeep. Taxis were in much greater abundance too and it was no longer necessary to queue interminably at special ranks or at hotels; it had become permitted to hail them in the street. I was surprised that the fares had risen quite so dramatically until it was explained to me that the particular taxi I was using was more expensive because it had air-conditioning. That fact that it was mid-winter and well below freezing didn't seem to lower the price any! With the increase in taxis came a greater demand for drivers, not all of whom seemed particularly qualified! Our worst experience ever was in Shanghai: it was quite late in the evening and the only taxi available was a small minibus. On the surface the driver appeared quite normal, but once behind the wheel…! Jekyll and Hyde had nothing on this man. Driving partly on main roads and partly down side streets, his speed never for one moment dropped below fifty mph, not even when negotiating narrow lanes in the dark and having to swerve violently to avoid old ladies, dogs and children. I had never before seen people literally throw themselves out of the path of an oncoming car, nor had I ever been quite so convinced that I was about to die. The sounds of screeching tyres were frequently punctuated by an insane giggling from the driver as he shouted, in broken English, "Big car. Big car". Had we been cats we would have lost several of our nine lives that night.

Think of Chinese roads and you think of bicycles – and there were thousands of them streaming past you at every turn (a count taken in 1980 at one of the busiest crossroads in the city reached 27,000 an hour at peak times). The original bike imported in to China had large wheels and all those produced in the country thereafter seemed to have been made to the same pattern in spite of the fact that they were far too big for the average Chinese rider, whose feet could not touch the ground. Because of that they developed the amazing skill of being able to ride at less than a snail's pace to avoid dismounting at a red light. If they had to stop they would make for the nearest pole or lamp post to hang on to until the lights changed – you could often see several people all clutching on to the same pole like maypole dancers on wheels. Mounting the bikes needed a fair amount of ingenuity and skill too: you scooted along with one foot on a pedal and the other on the ground until you had got up enough speed to swing yourself onto the bike. Even quite young children managed these enormous machines – either by standing up astride the crossbar or leaning to one side with both legs under the crossbar. The whole thing would have been made a lot easier if women's bikes, having no crossbars, had been available. All the bikes were incredibly heavy – great for withstanding the many knocks and crashes they were subjected to during their long lifespans – and all appeared identical, not helped by the fact that they were all black. There were in fact several different brands, the most popular being the romantically named Phoenix, Everlasting and Flying Pigeon. It never ceased to amaze me the things that people used to transport on the back of an ordinary bicycle: not just a friend or a child, but armchairs, settees, fridges, electric fans, exhaust pipes – you name it they'd try to strap it on the back. Some things just would not fit, in which case you resorted to using the other popular form of pedalled conveyance – the tricycle. Most of them had a flat wooden platform behind the rider and between the rear wheels onto which it was possible to pile an entire houseful of furniture. These 'flatbeds' also served as 'do-it-yourself' ambulances to take people to hospital: if the patient's head was nearest to the cyclist then he was alive, if his head was the other end he was dead. Another form of tricycle had an armchair in place of the wooden platform, and provided a very comfortable ride for an elderly person or an invalid. Children too small to ride for themselves were usually transported in little wooden sidecars attached to the side of a normal two-wheeler, and I even saw one or two hand-propelled bikes for the disabled and one with very home-made stabiliser wheels on the back for an old man who couldn't keep his balance.

One problem with all the bikes looking the same and being the same colour was recognising your own. At all the major shopping areas, parks and attractions, large areas were roped off as bicycle parks. On entering the area you paid the attendant a few *fen* (cents)and in return were issued with two identically numbered tickets – one to attach to your bike and one to keep with you. No one could remove a bike from under the watchful eye of the attendant without showing both matching tickets. I suspect it might well also have been the only sure way to leave with the bike you'd arrived on.

The sound of bicycle bells will always carry me back to Beijing – they being the most essential part of any bike and used almost constantly. The bells themselves were of a unique design: when the lever was depressed the whole of the top half of the bell rotated, hitting the stationary striker many times, thereby producing not one short ring as ours did, but the very long, protracted noise so necessary in the confusion of traffic, bicycles and pedestrians.

From the age of seven I tried to ride a bike, but with singular lack of success: no great handicap until I found myself in a nation of cyclists and exciting places inaccessible by car. An American teacher at the International School provided the solution when he sold me his Chinese tricycle, the type with the armchair behind. It proved to be absolutely wonderful and a great source of amusement to the locals, many of whom were so busy looking at me that they very nearly crashed into each other. The same teacher and his wife rode a tandem, and on one occasion were overtaken by a young man who ignored their shouts of warning but kept pedalling fast whilst staring back at them. As his bike came up short on the roadworks he soared gracefully on through the air. Buying a second-hand bike had the great advantage that the inevitable teething problems of all new ones in China had been sorted out by the previous owner, but had the disadvantage that I couldn't apply for a bike licence (all bikes were licensed) until my tricycle was first inspected. Hoping that my mastery of Chinese was up to the level of the traffic police, bicycle division, I turned down the offer of help from the Embassy and, map in hand, set off on the hour's ride to the test centre. I had to stop once to ask directions of a grandfather standing watching the world go by and from then on the 'jungle telegraph' took over – whenever I came to a turning or a crossroads there was invariably someone there pointing out the direction I should take. The paperwork at the testing station took but a few minutes and was dealt with in the first office I came to, but although the forms were filled in there, they had to be stamped after the inspection by another office. To kill two birds with one stone the policeman suggested that he rode the tricycle himself to the other side of the large compound, thereby testing it en route and passing on the forms at the same time. That, however, left the foreigner (me) in the wrong place, at the wrong side of the compound, so with an amused grin he offered me a ride in the seat at the back of my own tricycle. We set off to loud cheers and applause from his colleagues, who suggested he might always get a second job picking up passengers outside the railway station. The episode put everyone in a good mood – and I got my licence.

For those few people without bikes, or wishing to travel longer distances within the city, there was a good network of local buses – there just didn't seem to be enough of them! As London buses are double-decker to carry more passengers, the Beijing bus was double the length, but so as to remain manoeuvrable round corners, the middle section was a rubber concertina-like 'hinge'. The one thing the local population seemed totally incapable of doing was queuing. And to see a crowd of people waiting at a bus stop belied the scrum that ensued upon the bus's arrival. The minute it had stopped there were no holds barred and sharp elbows were weapons to be wielded mercilessly. Those passengers wishing to alight had to fight hard to do so against the sea of boarding commuters. The more agile young men had developed a method of ensuring access – albeit only possible in the summer months. As soon as the bus had stopped they ran round to the other side, clasped the top of the window frame and swung themselves athletically through the window opening.

A mode of transport that had been closed to foreigners, but which we were later allowed to use was the Underground. The circular route followed pretty closely the line of the old city walls, many of the bricks of which had been used to build the tunnels when the walls were demolished. The trains and stations were very clean and the one nearest to our flats boasted colourful murals. The name of each station was very clearly displayed in 'pinyin', making it one of the easier forms of transport for foreigners, as you always knew where you were, and the stations served all the main shopping areas and places of interest. The flat-rate fares were also very cheap and the common practice of charging the foreigner double hadn't caught on at that time, but, rather like Japan but a little less crowded, it was to be avoided at all costs during the rush hours or on Sundays. It was normal for foreigners to be charged a much higher fare on planes, trains, boats etc. but the explanation for this was that we were in fact paying the full fare, whereas the Chinese people were subsidised by the government, as their incomes were far below ours.

The tedious business of obtaining permission to travel, necessary in the 'early days', was thankfully discontinued and a large number of cities were designated open to foreigners – all that was needed was to book yourself on a plane or train. If, after seemingly endless searching, you were fortunate enough to find the right ticket office at the station, it was almost guaranteed that it was either shut or that it would close the minute you had worked your way to the front of the very long queue. Obtaining tickets for more distant destinations could literally take days of repeated returning to the station; so much so that it was rumoured that an enterprising young man had set himself up in an hotel room, offering to obtain tickets for a fee. We were fortunate enough to have Chinese staff at the Embassy who organised such things for us – and invaluable they were to. I can well remember a friend staying with us and trying to obtain a Mongolian visa – not too difficult a task one would have thought as the Mongolian Embassy was just around the corner from us, and the opening times were on a notice at the gate. They had, however, found a novel way to limit the number of visas issued and the amount of work involved in issuing them – they kept changing the opening times. It would state quite clearly that visa applications were accepted on Mondays, Wednesdays and Fridays from 11 to 12 and 3.30 to 5, but when you turned up at one of those times the days and times had all been changed, and when you tried again at the new times, they too had been altered in your absence. The only way to be sure of getting any attention at all was to wait until they changed the notices and follow them back inside!

Once you had your tickets it was necessary to arrive early at the station as all the train departure information was posted in characters, and the information desk always seemed to be manned by someone with a very strong (Chinese) accent that I could hardly understand. After a maze of corridors crowded with passengers, you usually found yourself in a large square waiting area with seats, and toilet facilities off to one side. All the seats would be jammed full and the floor littered with children, or even whole families, lying down on blankets or duvets. The Chinese had a great and enviable ability to curl up and sleep anywhere. Those areas were naturally cleared every time a train departed, but outside the station itself families slept on the ground for one or two days waiting for a train.

Boarding the train was far less traumatic, as all seats booked were numbered and heaven preserve you from the wrath of the attendant should you sit in someone else's. There were two classes on Chinese trains: 'hard' and 'soft', and the difference really was just that, either hard seats or softly cushioned ones. The toilets were small and basically clean, at the start of the journey at least, and to ensure that they weren't used at stations (they emptied straight onto the track) the carriage attendant would lock the toilet door. Each carriage had several attendants who were constantly sweeping, checking on the passengers and pouring boiling water from large metal kettles into your teacup. Should your journey be an overnight one you could either enjoy a very social trip in a open plan, hard class sleeper (three bunks high, many rows per carriage) or luxuriate in soft class in a four berth compartment, complete with small table covered in a lace cloth plus a pot of flowers and thermos of hot water. It was 'roundabouts and swings', as you were on constant display in hard class, but couldn't choose your soft class companions and if you really couldn't stand them there was no way of escape. Male and female of the same party were all expected to share the same compartment, and on one occasion Mike and I had to share with two middle aged Chinese men, who were so 'proper' they even slept with their hats on. It was usually possible to change into a tracksuit or, in winter, to strip off the top few layers and sleep on your long thermal underwear. Sleeper trains carried many more attendants than short haul ones, and included railway policemen, engineers and wheeltappers, who really did get out and tap the wheels at stations along the route, listening for any change of note that would indicate a crack or a fault. At regular intervals along the way announcements were made for the benefit of newly joined passengers and a reminder to those already embarked. These were the railway byelaws and there seemed to be hundreds of them covering just about anything that might occur: we were told all the things we were not allowed on the train, such as explosives and highly combustible material (there had been a nasty accident involving several deaths when someone inadvertently tossed a cigarette butt into a fellow passenger's open tin of paint thinner), and ordered not to allow our children to wet the beds or urinate on the floors but to use the toilets. The list of dos and don'ts seemed to go on forever, but was eventually replaced by loud music – we did manage to find a volume control, but there was no way to actually turn off the address system. At least we weren't expected to join our fellow passengers on the platform at dawn to participate in the exercises, but having been woken up by the loud 'encouragement' from the attendant (did anyone ever dare not get up?) we stood in the corridor and watched. Whilst we were all thus engaged our beds were stripped and the floors washed, although we were not due in to our final destination for several hours.

Food on long train journeys was an important part of the day, and was not charged for per dish but as a set meal, and with a choice of three different prices. The lowest seemed to cater for the 'it'll fill you up, but nothing special' brigade; the middle range gave a good variety of courses; and the most expensive tasted much the same but featured more exotic varieties of meat and fish. We always plumped for the middle price range, but even at that were on occasion served frogs' legs. Every dish was cooked fresh in a tiny corridor of a kitchen with flaming gas rings and enormous woks. The one dish I shall always associate with Chinese trains is egg and tomato soup. The first time we were served this was at the end of a particularly tasty lunch en route to Wuhan, soup traditionally being served at the end of the meal. As was the custom the Chinese passengers had been fed first and there were few diners left except for the crew. The soup was tasty, if rather greasy, and we were just serving ourselves from the large tureen placed in the middle of the table when the train made the quickest emergency stop known to man. None of the tables and chairs was attached to the floor in that part of the train and the whole lot started to slide. Bottles and glasses were saved by the swift actions of those sitting at tables, but there was nothing I could do as I saw a tureen load of soup heading straight for me. Fortunately, like all train food, it wasn't very hot, but as the train finally slid to a halt I found myself festooned with threads of egg and slices of tomato, and getting colder and greasier by the minute. There was tremendous embarrassment amongst the attendants – why had it had to happen to a foreigner – and in an effort to make amends one of them grabbed a cloth from the kitchen and attempted to wipe me down. Unfortunately, as most train cloths, it put on more grease than it took off, but of a different colour. We stoically finished our meal before returning to the compartment for a change of clothes. Any driver would naturally brake if he saw an obstruction on the line ahead (it was a cow in that instance), but he would be extra zealous in stopping quickly were it an attempted suicide – were the attempt successful the driver could be held liable. Several years later we were accompanying two 'official' guests on a sleeper and were served egg and tomato soup once again. As Mike was recounting our previous experience we were amazed to feel the train suddenly brake hard, and as if in a time warp the soup once more left the bowl and headed in my direction. Forewarned was forearmed – I grabbed the tablecloth as a shield while the others, with lightning speed, were upright and standing in the passageway out of the line of fire.

In the 'early days' in Hong Kong you could buy a tee-shirt with the logo 'CAAC Survivor', CAAC being the Civil Aviation Authority of China. It also bore a cartoon-like picture of an aeroplane with nuts, bolts and other essential items falling off and showering the people below. There was rather more truth in the characterisation than most travellers were happy with, and it was strongly rumoured that their statistically very low accident rate was because they only reported crashes that had involved foreigners or had been observed by them and they therefore couldn't hush up. Very few Chinese citizens had ever had, nor would they ever have, the opportunity to fly: only those on Party or Work Unit business would be able to do so, and to many it was a totally alien experience. Despite the fact that they quite clearly had numbered seats, the minute a flight was announced a scrum similar to that around a Beijing bus ensued. Once everyone was finally settled and seat belts were tied together (buckles often didn't work) the plane could take off and in-flight meals were served. These consisted of sandwiches and packs of dried meat rather like biltong which were quite literally thrown at you from the aisle, beer served in the bottle without a glass and tea poured from large aluminium kettles. As the time for landing approached some attempt at clearing up was made, although contents of overhead lockers still spilled out occasionally, which became positively dangerous if flying back from Hainan Island and the majority of passengers had brought bags of coconuts home. No checks on seat belts were made, but then the stewardesses didn't bother to wear them either. Many of the pilots seemed to have been transferred from the Air Force, if their way of approaching the runway was anything to go by, as they seemed to keep to a steady height until the runway was in sight and then dived steeply as if on a bombing raid. Quite literally the moment the wheels touched the ground the passengers were up out of their seats, grabbing their hand baggage and queuing along the aisle to be amongst the first to disembark. It quite worried them that we stayed seated and they would go to great lengths to explain to us that we had arrived and it was time to get off.

There were rules governing type and size of hand baggage – at Kai Tak airport in Hong Kong your bags were actually measured and often refused, but CAAC turned a very blind eye! A large lorry exhaust pipe was but one of many objects we encountered lying unsecured in an aisle, but the most unusual must have been the extremely large and very belligerent turtle which suddenly appeared under the seats and started to nip at the heels of the passengers. Hearing the ensuing commotion, a stewardess fiercely berated the owner, who put the creature back in its polythene bag. Within minutes it had eaten its way out again, so the woman tried to knock it unconscious by banging its head on an armrest until she was told that it would not only make a mess of the seat but would upset the foreign passengers. The problem was finally solved by a passenger from Hong Kong who produced a much higher quality carrier bag made of thick, turtle-proof plastic.

There were some much more serious lapses in safety procedures: Mike was in a flight whose takeoff was delayed and the stewardess announced that the pilot didn't like the sound of the starboard engine, but that they only had to wait until they could find a pilot who did! On one flight I found myself sitting next to an American engineer who had in-depth knowledge of the engines fitted to our plane: he spent the whole flight nervously telling me in great detail every fault he could hear. The story of both pilot and co-pilot leaving the cockpit, getting locked out and having to break in using a hatchet might well be true, but the most frightening near-disaster was actually witnessed by Mike at Beijing airport. Standing in the car park, he saw a small 'executive' plane coming in to land and, to his horror, just behind it and closing fast a large passenger jet preparing to land on the same runway at the same time. It was one of those awful nightmare moments of inevitability and helplessness: there was no way of averting disaster on time. At what seemed to be the last possible moment the pilot of the larger plane spotted the other one in his path, pulled up fast and screamed off into the air.

Apart from the natural concerns over your safety, flying at that time could be very frustrating. Booking a seat was hard enough and over-booking quite a common problem, but one that was often easily solved by 'borrowing' folding chairs from the airport restaurant and putting them in the aisle for the excess passengers. Delays occurred for all manner of reasons including the use of the runway by local peasants to spread out their grain to dry, it being a large, clean area of tarmac. Often if waiting for an incoming flight it would suddenly disappear from the arrivals board without explanation, hopefully to reappear up to a couple of hours later. When a limit was put on CAAC of only one direct flight from Hong Kong to Beijing per day, passengers would suddenly find themselves landing unexpectedly at Tianjin airport where they had to disembark and eat a meal. With the minimum of delay the plane was reloaded and took off for Beijing – only with a different flight number, so no longer being a direct flight according to the rules. There was just one time when getting a seat on a plane was really easy, and that was as a result of a highjacking attempt. It was immediately announced that only the most senior Party members would be allowed to fly, and there weren't an awful lot of them. Mind you, the empty seats weren't wasted, they were simply piled high with freight. Hijackings were virtually unheard of: not only were the penalties so severe, but the fellow passengers were a force to be reckoned with. One man who attempted to take over a plane was attacked by some of his fellow travellers and knocked unconscious with a beer bottle. There was great talk afterwards of moral principles and doing the right thing but I always suspected that the passengers had suffered so much in the booking of tickets, delays and frustrations that there was no way on earth that they were going to let anyone interfere with their journey.

One of the most welcome changes to take place during our absence from China was the complete overhaul of CAAC. Cabin crew seemed aware of the dangers of passengers walking around during landing, unsecured baggage and kettles of boiling water. It all became much more sophisticated and inspired a great deal more confidence. Whether the planes themselves received as much attention remains to be seen, but I certainly worried a lot less about flying in them.

No matter what the mode of transport, adverse weather conditions were inclined to bring them to a virtual standstill. Because of the very dry atmosphere in winter there was little snow, but should any fall, cars ground to a halt whilst bicycles fared better, as the cycle tracks were swept clear. To guard against frozen radiators, buses and lorries were fitted with padded bonnet covers, although should temperatures drop drastically the drivers would empty the radiators every night – usually over the road, where the water soon froze into a lethal stream of ice. Camels of course didn't have such problems, and as late as the early 1900s they were still being used around the city to transport coal and wood. They had originally been introduced by the Mongolians going to the Imperial Court on business, and proved so useful that their numbers soon increased, although they couldn't be used in the summer months because of the intense heat. The villagers who owned the camels (often an entire village's economy was based on them) treated them very well, and when they got too old to work (the camels that is) they were sold off to the Muslims as meat. Sure beats a scrap yard full of old cars!

Chapter Eight: Everyday Life...As We Saw It

From our modern, luxuriously furnished, flat we could see the roofs of the Forbidden City and, on a clear day, the Western Hills, but in the foreground we enjoyed an even more interesting view over some of the many narrow lanes and rows of small houses populated by the local residents. These lanes dated from the 1200s when the Mongols ruled Beijing and the name for them, 'hutong', is a Mongol word. There were around 3,000 hutongs in the city and many bore fascinating names such as Small Sheep Pen Hutong, Brick Pagoda Hutong, Cooked White Rice Hutong and Twisting Way Hutong. Occasionally they were named after a famous person who had lived there. The hutongs, some tarmac'd, others simply stones and beaten earth, were lined with doorways, through which it was sometimes possible to see a small courtyard with either a row, or more usually a square, of small, single-storey houses grouped around it. 'Houses' is something of a misnomer, as they were very small. The courtyards themselves were mostly full of stored cabbages, boxes, pots and pans, bicycles and sometimes a small area of earth dug over for a miniscule vegetable patch. Washing hung out on lines and circular coal briquettes made from compacted coal dust were neatly piled in corners. If there wasn't enough hanging space inside the courtyard then heavy cotton duvets in the winter and thin towelling bed covers in the summer would be hung out to air on ropes strung between the trees lining the streets. Despite the lack of space and the all-pervading dust and dirt, everything was spotlessly clean and the occupants' clothes and general appearance immaculate. This was all the more amazing when you realised that there was no running water to the houses: it had to be fetched from a communal tap in the street or, if you were fortunate, in the courtyard itself, and then heated up over a coal stove. The tiny houses were often just two rooms with the cooking on the coal stove done in the living area. The stove itself also helped to heat the house: the flue would be very long and snaked around the room just below the ceiling, thus acting as a radiator. It eventually led through a small hole to the outside where a little tin bucket was hung over the end to stop tar dripping onto the pavement. In the depths of the bitterly cold Beijing winter it was often warmer outside in the sunshine than in the house and you would see children playing outside, wrapped up like mini 'Michelin men', and heaven protect them from the wrath of 'granny' should they shed a layer of clothing. We caused amazement by not wearing as many thick clothes, but when we went home to our centrally heated, double-glazed flat we could quickly warm up, whereas they couldn't: once chilled they risked staying that way. In the summer months these hutong houses could become unbearably hot, so once the sun had gone for the day the occupants would often sit outside in the cooler air, grouped under streetlamps, reading or chatting. A few people even moved beds outside onto the cool grass – even if it was on the verge of a three lane highway.

Not only were the water taps communal – so were the toilets. There was one at the end of every street: a brick building with the men's toilet one end and the ladies' the other. Near the roof were open window spaces for ventilation which meant the unheated building was very cold and draughty in winter – not a place to linger. You could always find a toilet in the hutongs – just follow your nose! Although they were kept very clean and well-swept they were, by their very design, incredibly smelly. They were basically a concrete or tiled trough running the length of the building, over which was placed a concrete slab with 3 or 4 rectangular holes in it. Sometimes the holes had ceramic linings, but often times not. In some cases a small half-wall formed a partition between the holes but many were just 'open plan', and none of them ever had a door. Should you be carrying, as in my case, a small child, there was nowhere to put him down so I always waited a few minutes for another person to arrive. Whilst obligingly carrying Jonathan, a lady once asked me in great detail if all foreigners wore 'that type of underwear'. The smell was caused by the fact that you couldn't flush them – they just had a fetid puddle at the bottom. They were periodically flushed out into a holding tank in the ground but unlike our septic tanks this contained no chemicals; it was just raw sewage. I originally thought the lack of flushing was to preserve water in the very dry climate, but it was more likely that the sewage shouldn't be 'watered down' as it was used as manure. This so-called 'night soil' was regularly sucked out of the holding tanks into small tanker lorries and then spread onto the arable land around the city. We might find this an unacceptable procedure but is there *really* such a difference between using animal or human waste on the very infertile soil? It certainly seemed to work well: one commune I visited grew wonderful produce on the principle of planting so close together that not a patch of earth showed (none of this so many inches between plants and rows!) and using lashings of fertiliser. In the countryside the toilets were even more basic, some being nothing more than a wattle fence around a few holes dug in the earth – all very public, but far less smelly – and no truck, night soil being removed and carried in wooden buckets.

To use the toilets you had to develop incredible balance to allow you to crouch down without either falling down the hole or developing excruciating pins and needles. This ability came in very useful too when subjected to a lengthy wait at a bus stop, as you could just crouch down and relax for an indefinite time – a position which most Westerners found far from restful after the first couple of minutes. It was surprising how quickly you became used to the toilets and thought of them as quite normal. I well remember the horror of one visitor at the state of the toilets she was shown to on a tour of China: they were in fact spotless, but to achieve that they had literally been hosed out floor to ceiling just before the 'honoured foreign guests' arrived – what water didn't slosh around your feet, dripped copiously down upon you from above. With more Western visitors many hotels, restaurants and even shops installed 'our' type of conveniences, but if a Chinese woman had to use one she would as often as not still crouch in the traditional way by standing on the toilet seat. The desire for good night soil (and inadequate sewage pipes) still stuck in the mind for many a year too, and used toilet paper wouldn't be allowed to contaminate the sewage, but was thrown into an open wire basket on the floor. I read a wonderful quote once – "Half the population of China finds occupation in transporting the excrements of the other half."

Looking out over the hutongs from our flat we could see the whole of life: children going off to school, adults cycling off to work, grandmothers taking babies and toddlers out for a walk, a knife grinder and saucepan repair man of great age calling out for custom whilst wheeling his even older bike festooned with all manner of paraphernalia and the tools of his trade. We sometimes heard, in the very early morning, what sounded to be a 'waker-upper', making sure none overslept. In older times a watchman would patrol the streets all night sounding out the hours on bamboo clappers and making enough noise to scare off evil spirits of this world and the next.

In the past the wealthier Chinese families used to enjoy far roomier accommodation in 'courtyard houses': single storey pavilions built around a central courtyard and often housing a very extended family of many generations, together with servants. In addition the richer families would often employ a gatekeeper, or 'kaimendi', who was more than just a humble watchman – he levied taxes on anything and everything that passed through 'his' gate. Eggs costing maybe 2 fen would be charged to the family at 6 fen, the profit supplementing the kaimendi's wages. Depending on the size of the courtyard, trees and flowers were grown, giving a communal garden area. Some of these splendid buildings were still in existence, but you seldom had a chance to peek inside as immediately behind the main entrance was a 'spirit screen'. Evil spirits can only travel in straight lines so can be prevented from entering your home by erecting a short section of wall, often painted and decorated, across the entrance, just behind the doorway. It was also the practice to build a wooden or stone step across many of the doorways of the individual houses, and you should always step over, not on, this.

With the equality of the Communist system no families retained sole use of their 'ancestral' homes, and the many units of the courtyard housing would be allocated to many families rather than just one. That naturally gave rise to problems if the various occupants didn't get along together and argued over the use, or misuse, of the communal courtyard areas. Sadly both courtyard and hutong housing was disappearing as they were compulsorily purchased, demolished, and blocks of flats built in their place: flats which belonged to the government. No one was allowed to buy a place of their own, and you had limited choice as to where you lived, although it was possible sometimes (and often after a bit of a battle) to change your allotted flat. With the desperate housing shortage, demolition and rebuilding was an obvious solution and it was successful in that it provided not only more housing but a much better standard of living with running water, heating and toilets. Mind you, the water only came in cold, the heating was only switched on for certain hours and the toilets were shared by two or more flats. It might have seemed antiquated to us, but it must have seemed wonderfully convenient after life in a hutong, although I heard of some people experiencing exactly the problems that occurred in Britain with the onset of high-rises – loneliness. At least living in the old way you always saw your neighbours about, and the children could run in and out freely, whereas the new Beijing housing was far from convenient for the majority of those home all day, being the elderly and very young, neither of whom could easily manage stairs. There was also an increasing problem, with the emergence of a more affluent society, of theft and no built-in 'neighbourhood watch' as there had been in the close-knit hutong communities. If your flat was on the ground floor it became almost essential to have bars fitted over the windows, and you would certainly not leave bicycles outside at night: imagine sharing two small rooms not only with maybe four or five family members but with their bicycles as well. Loss of the outside storage areas found in the hutongs meant that all manner of boxes, cabbages etc, were piled up either on balconies or on the staircases: a great fire risk and an even greater danger to life and limb as there were often no light bulbs working, and in the darkness it was all too easy to fall over these piles of possessions. To partially combat the fire danger was the advantage of easier access for emergency services to flats rather than narrow lanes, and although the ladders seemed rather short, the blocks weren't very high. The exception were the diplomatic housing blocks, but the Chief of the Beijing Fire Service was the tallest man I had ever met, so I lived in the hope that he might make up the 'shortfall'! (At one time Chinese fire engines were not allowed access into the diplomatic housing compounds, but sense eventually prevailed.)

Reactions to the new housing were mixed – some loved the modern convenience whilst others regretted the disappearance of the old ways, especially those whose courtyard homes had been in their families for generations, and who were then moved a long way outside the centre of the city, making contact with friends, and travel to work, arduous.

Fortunately not all the old buildings were demolished, and there was a sudden appearance of white marble plaques on doorways declaring a building 'protected'. Many were restored, repainted and returned to their former glory, but unfortunately there wasn't enough money to allow them all to be thus restored. On occasion 'protected' merely meant it couldn't be demolished, but it could be left to fall down on its own. I found a set of old maps of Beijing showing the vast numbers of temples once in existence, many of which I was pleased to discover were still standing, but used as schools or offices. It was interesting to discover that the Jianguo Hotel was built on the site of the tomb of a member of the Imperial family and one of the diplomatic housing compounds, Qi Jia Yuan, was originally the Qi family's garden. There was talk that during some previous building work at the British Embassy bones were unearthed in the garden.

Along with the policy of preservation was an ongoing 'green' campaign. Chairman Mao had come to the conclusion that grass harboured mosquitoes, so he had all grass removed, which unfortunately led to widespread soil erosion and swirling dust every time the wind blew. To redress the balance there was finally a great move to replant the grass, build gardens and plant trees, an evolution that involved everyone from schoolchildren to soldiers. There were tree planting days when every school, college, work unit, office or factory was expected to 'do their bit', but this tree planting bore little resemblance to the gardening we were used to: no tender saplings tended for years until big enough to plant out; in Beijing full-sized trees, their roots wrapped in sacking, were delivered by lorry and were put straight into the very large holes prepared for them. Enormous quantities of water were then poured over the earth which, far from drowning the trees, seemed to ensure a healthy start, for I never saw one die. Opposite our flat, between the new ring road and the hutongs was a patch of bare earth left from the construction of the road. One day a team of workers arrived and drew out shapes on the earth, to be followed the following day by a veritable army of men and women wielding shovels. Within a few weeks we looked out onto the beginnings of a beautiful garden with flowerbeds, shrubs, trees, paths and a fountain and small pond. After a mere six months it was fully established and provided a place for all the locals to congregate. In the summer especially it gave welcome coolness, but the fountain and pond had to be drained for health reasons as so many children were paddling or lying down in it.

Chairman Mao could not be held responsible for all the dust in the city: the amount of coal used by households and in industry gave rise to a great deal of air pollution, and what we knew as dust in the U.K., in Beijing was gritty, black and sooty and seemed to get in through any crack in any door or window frame. Not only did it make everything grey, it also gave everything a smoky smell and clothes that we could normally have worn for two or three days needed to be washed after a few hours. Worse still than any of that, but fortunately confined to the Spring months, were the dust storms. You would suddenly see a dark cloud approaching as the wind got up and within minutes sand and dust from as far away as the Gobi Desert obliterated everything further than a few feet away, while the sun turned the most amazing blue colour. Sandy grit got everywhere, and if you were unfortunate enough to be caught outside it was like being sandblasted. Grit got into your eyes, nose, mouth and ears – it was real 'hide behind your camel' stuff, but having no camels to hide behind, the locals had developed their own unique way of avoiding some of the discomfort if unable to run for cover. By completely covering your head with a thin chiffon scarf (any amazing, bright colour) and tying it securely around your neck you cut out 90% of the sand whilst remaining able to see. Once again, sense overcame vanity: how much better to avoid eyes full of grit than to care about looking like an alien human/fly.

It wasn't just the housing and living conditions that differed from our own: as a Chinese citizen your whole life was virtually ruled by the

Communist Party in the wide aspect and by your *'danwei'*, or work unit, on a more local level, but even from a very early age you were a part of the 'system'. For a woman to work was a necessity in most households, just to earn enough to keep a couple solvent, and when the time came for the woman to be given permission to become pregnant, she would take as little maternity leave as possible. As couples were often allocated jobs in separate provinces, childcare could have created a problem were it not for the extended family. Many work units had nurseries and crèches, but it was also very common for a mother to have very little to do with the upbringing of her child, handing that responsibility over to retired grandparents. There appeared to be no feeling of loss, as when the mother herself became a granny she'd then have the pleasure of bringing up a baby (albeit her grandchild, not her child). Babies and toddlers were pushed around in bamboo prams – double-ended affairs with handles at both ends. They had a myriad of uses: as pram, pushchair (add two seats and a plank table between), as a shopping trolley or gas bottle transporter when the children started school, and as a kind of zimmer frame on wheels for the elderly and infirm. There were still some old ladies to be seen with bound feet, a practice which began almost 1,000 years ago because small feet were considered beautiful. At a wedding in the past the bride's face would be covered with a red scarf, but her feet in their tiny embroidered shoes would be displayed so that everyone could marvel at their beauty (i.e. size). Because of every mother's fear that her daughter would never find a husband if her feet were normal size, any attempt to stop the awful practice of foot-binding failed. It was as late as 1919 that it was to disappear forever. Not only did it make the everyday chores of cleaning, cooking, caring for many children and even working in the fields extremely arduous and painful, but it also in old age could be a contributory factor in ill-health, as women with bound feet often put on weight and their unsteadiness caused falls and broken bones.

Slightly older children were at kindergarten, where they lived for six days (and nights) a week. They were often taken out to the parks by white-coated kindergarten assistants, as there was inadequate space within the schools themselves for them to run around and let off stream.

To keep them all safe and under control en route they walked in pairs, crocodile-fashion, but were all 'tied' together. One adult held the end of a long rope which had pairs of small loops attached at intervals along its length, and each child slipped its wrist through one of the loops, the rear being brought up by another lady helper. No matter what the age of the child, it never seemed to occur to them to slip free. Sundays the children would spend with their families and although the system might seem rather hard to us, the children were brought up that way and naturally thought of it as quite normal. The schools I saw were lacking in comfort, having bare floors and basic furniture, but what they lacked in 'modcons' was more than made up for in the high teacher/pupil ratio. Even university students weren't given any luxury, or even much comfort, surviving in very cold buildings with no hot water – it was hard to write with gloves on.

Schooling was taken very seriously by the children and by their parents, who realised how much had been lost during the last years of the Cultural Revolution. All schooling stopped then, although some basic lessons still took place undercover out in the fields where the teachers had been sent to 'learn from the peasants'. The effect of these 'lost years' showed itself not just amongst the academics, but amongst the manual trades as well: there were many old electricians, plumbers etc. and many young inexperienced apprentices, but no one in between. One elderly father expressed regret that his three children all worked in factories although capable of much more: they were 'children of the Cultural Revolution' who had missed the most important years of their education. Any chance of extra lessons, night school etc. was taken, and when I taught English my students asked why they had to have Sundays off.

Should a child show an unusual gift, be it musical or sporting, he or she might well have been transferred to a special school where a large proportion of the school day was spent developing the child's natural talents. This undoubtedly made for prize- and medal-winning athletes and performers, but did it make for happy, well-rounded children? On the whole it probably did, although one ex-Olympic gymnast who trained children from the age of four, said that she'd never allow her daughter to undergo the specialised and narrow education and training that she herself had experienced.

During our first year in China (1981) I was sometimes asked why I was allowed more than one child. In certain cases in China, such as in rural areas where workers were needed on the land, and minority peoples who would otherwise be in danger of dying out, more than one child was permitted, but for the majority a second child meant great loss of privileges and a large fine. Reportedly a second pregnancy, surely almost always intentional given the freely available contraception and sterilisation, could result in a forced abortion, but I never heard a Chinese person verify, deny or even mention it. My explanations of the U.K.'s more static population and the dangers of overpopulation as regards feeding alone, let alone medical and educational services, all sounded rather hollow coming from the mother of two. To the old way of thinking it was vital to have male children, as only males could worship the ancestors (i.e. yourself, after your death). Also males stayed within the family, eventually bringing wives into the communal home as servants. Girls, on the other hand, had to be married off and then became totally the property of the husband's family. Years back girls and boys were often separated once over four years old and one of the principle occupations of the girls seemed to be to sit at home and embroider their trousseaux. The Chinese nationality generally looked upon daughters as misfortunes and gave them no privileges, whereas the Manchus, although they preferred sons, treated their female children very differently. Whilst unmarried they were as important within the family as their brothers and were certainly considered more important than their sisters-in-law (differentiating between natural relations and acquired ones). Manchu girls also had some rights as to property and greater freedom as regards marriage and choice of partner. Those fortunate ladies did not have their feet bound either. Later on, in 1987, I discussed the one child policy with several young people, who all agreed that it was better to have one fit, well-fed and educated child than to become like many third world countries where children died of starvation and disease simply because there were just too many of them. Further incentives were also being given at that time to encourage couples to promise to have one child and to marry late. The annual holiday for a man who married after the age of 25 and a woman after the age of 23, was increased from 15 days to 22. A single child family was subsidised until the child was 14, and received an annual payment roughly equivalent to one month's wages. Should a woman delay having a child until she was over the age of 24 she was given 71 days maternity leave instead of 56, and that could be extended to 6 months or a year on full pay, but with no subsidies. A lot of facts and figures, but more holidays and especially more money were enormous incentives to couples to toe the Party line.

The one growing fear generally expressed was that the single child (especially boys) was becoming increasingly spoilt, and adored like a 'Little Emperor', not just because he was the only child a couple would have but also because with higher standards of living, there was the feeling of needing to give your child all the things you never had yourself. There were articles in newspapers and magazines enjoining parents and grandparents to avoid spoiling children. To the Western point of view loneliness seemed to be a probable problem with all the single children, but the system of residential kindergartens and some primary schools as well, meant that they in fact grew up in an enormous 'family' of peers who were like brothers and sisters to them. A further problem may well arise in the future however: previously the burden of care of sick or elderly parents was shared between many children, but in time it will all fall upon one child, and should the child be a girl who marries and leaves the home for good, then there is no one to care for her parents. Some homes for such elderly people had already started to appear in Beijing in the late 80s, and many more might well be needed in the times to come. (In olden times there was no great burden of care for the elderly as you were supposedly buried alive if you lived past the age of 60!)

Once you graduated from school the system really took over. When Mrs. Yuan's eldest daughter qualified as a middle school teacher, she wasn't given the opportunity of looking for a job of her choice but was assigned one by the State. This served to solve the problem of filling vacancies in unpopular or remote areas, but hardly made for a happy work environment, as very often the new employee was miserable and the local people often resented outsiders coming in. Nor were there any great incentives to actually volunteer for such positions, although there was plenty to 'encourage' you to accept gratefully and see it through to the end! Should you have been assigned to Tibet you were expected to stay there for eight years before asking to be moved, whereas if you actually offered to go there you would receive – praise! Failure to turn up for your new job within 90 days resulted in your forfeiting the right to work, and you would be blacklisted by all major employers for 5 years. I guess in that situation any employment, no matter how unpopular, was better than none. As with all societies, no matter how idealistic, there was always the 'back door', either through contacts or payments, to getting the position you wanted for yourself or someone in your family. As a preventative measure, those parents likely to help their offspring in that way (i.e. those with money or social standing or political power) were invited to attend special meetings to 'explain the rules' to them. The back door was increasingly becoming a problem as the general wealth of the population increased, and the greater the desires to ensure a comfortable lifestyle.

From the minute you started work you came under the auspices of one particular work unit, or 'danwei'. These were more than merely divisions of the labour force, they were more like exclusive clubs – but with compulsory membership and enforced rules. They allocated you your job, paid your wages, and generally told you what to do – to the extent, I heard, of informing you of the decision on your application to get married or have a child. Without belonging to a work unit you could not register for employment, benefits, housing etc. and were not free to move to another city to work unless you had their approval. They also dealt with health problems or hospitalisation, protected you from the worry of unemployment – and issued occasional theatre tickets! The danwei was the main line of communication between individual citizens and the

Communist Party, a responsibility which they took very seriously. The villages may have been far removed in distance and time from the cities, but the government still managed to keep a pretty strict eye on the inhabitants through street committees and Party representatives. Urgent, important messages and propaganda were broadcast to the entire village through loudspeakers. It seemed the only ones outwith the net were itinerant bee keepers who were forever moving their hives and tent-like shelters from one good source of pollen to another: or maybe there were itinerant Party members to keep their eye on them!

The one thing I noticed particularly about work in China was that, although given no real choice of work or location, there appeared to be complete sexual equality and you'd as likely see a woman driving a bus or a lorry as a man. There was also no unemployment (said the Party), only those 'awaiting employment', although the wait was obviously long enough for some young people to try to move independently from the country to the cities in hopes of finding casual work. Unattached to a danwei and finding the streets were not paved with gold, some of them became so impoverished that they all too easily turned to a life of petty crime. Any who found themselves 'awaiting' didn't appear to be allowed to sit back idly but would be employed somehow. One disadvantage was that you were in danger of suffering from the 'too many cooks' syndrome by having two or three people doing what was basically a one person job. It was a joke amongst the foreign community that two people came to read your gas and electricity meters because one could read and one could write!

Unlike many countries, arranged marriages as such had ceased to exist under Communism, although parents could make it very difficult for a child to marry against their wishes. At one time many newly-weds had been in debt for the first five or more years of married life simply trying to pay off the costs of the reception, a lavish affair with hundreds of guests; so the government had a drive at persuading couples to cut out the over-expensive ceremonies and entertaining and go for a far simpler affair – or even to split the costs with three or more other couples and have a joint wedding.

At least the old ideas of the 'ideal woman' were no longer a prerequisite in a fiancée. Previously she had to be virtuous, discreet in her speech, tidy and diligent. And if that were not enough, she had the '3 obeys' to worry about: as a girl she had to obey her father; as a wife, her husband; as a mother, her children. Nor did the obligations stop there – once she'd proved herself a good wife she had to succeed as a mother, and she had '3 obligations' towards any girls born to her: to bind their feet, to pierce their ears and to marry them off.

It wasn't all that long ago that such traditions were accepted as the norm, but if you'd been born into a practising Confucian family of the past your life would have been really restrictive, as their codes were based on the lifestyle of the original Kong family (Kong Fu Zi being the Chinese name that we anglicised to Confucius). His whole ethos was a simple and scholarly life, and to ensure ensuing family members followed suit even the children were dressed very plainly and were kept virtually cut off from the outside world. They were not even allowed outside the family home. Nothing modern was allowed to them, not even such 'harmless' things as thermos flasks and pens, and certainly no glass mirrors. (Chinese mirrors were originally highly polished brass). Unless it was absolutely unavoidable nothing new was ever purchased and things handed down from the ancestors were deemed precious and had to be kept, which meant that you only possessed articles they had favoured and no matter how much you might hate them, they could not be thrown away. Children were taught by tutors inside the Mansion, but most of what you learnt was simply by rote and independent thinking was positively discouraged. The tutors instructed their charges in social skills as well as academic subjects and were so well respected that they could exert a certain amount of influence over children's upbringing (even to the extent of not permitting girls' feet to be bound). However much of an honour it might have been to be a Kong family tutor, it was a really full-time job and they seldom went home to their own families, living nearly all of their working lives with their pupils.

The whole Mansion was kept as part fortress, part mini empire. Where the women lived, no outside men were allowed: even the water was delivered into a trough outside the inner courtyard wall, which led through the wall to a second trough on the ladies' side. No matter how dire the emergency no rule could be broken, and a fire once raged for three days and nights and destroyed seven buildings because the male servants were not allowed entry to fight it. The servants themselves became almost members of the 'clan', often passing on their jobs from grandparents, through sons to grandsons – generations of a family holding the same position. At one time servants even changed their surnames to 'Kong' and were subject to the penal codes of the Mansion rather than of the country as a whole.

Confucius' original home in Qufu had only three rooms and was converted after his death to a temple. Over the years various Emperors enlarged the area until it boasted four hundred rooms and halls and was even topped with Imperial yellow roof tiles from Beijing. The ten carved dragon pillars erected in the main hall were said to be so superior to those of the Imperial palace that whenever the Emperor visited, the columns would have to be covered in yellow silk lest he become jealous: a far cry from those three simple rooms! The main purpose of the vastly enlarged Mansion became to offer sacrifices to Confucius, for which much of the surrounding land had to be rented or sold, and enough grain sold to finance these very costly ceremonies. With no other aim in mind there really was nothing to bring the place out if its stagnation. Even the Emperor would kowtow (kneel and touch your forehead to the floor three times) to Confucius' ancestors as he would to his own, and the current head of the Clan was the only person ever allowed to walk at the Emperor's side, so revered were the Kong family. Their graveyard, set in acres of woodland and being today the largest preserved private cemetery in China, boasted statuary on a par with that of the Imperial tombs, although Confucius' tomb was quite simple. Perhaps it was a good thing that the Kongs were blissfully unaware of the power they could have exerted outside the enclaves, had they been ambitious. Even as late as 1900, when a railway was being built nearby, it was feared that the spirit of Confucius might be disturbed, so the line made a great detour and Qufu has no railway station.

The founding of the Republic in 1911 meant that money previously received from the Emperor stopped, as did all Imperial gifts, and by the 1920s the Mansion was heading into dire financial straits, but being the totally unworldly place it was, not a single servant was dismissed and costly sacrifices continued. They ended up in debt, but the reverence in which they held anything bequeathed them by the ancestors prevented their selling off any of the numerous and valuable treasures. They slipped further and further down the slippery slope, not helped by an upsurge of the anti-Confucian movement. Help, when it came, was from an unusual direction: the Japanese invasion. Wanting to win over the Chinese people, they showed great and ostentatious reverence for Confucius by visiting the Mansion/temple to pay their respects, and make a donation. The names and amounts donated were written up where they were clearly visible to following worshippers, who would more than likely feel duty bound to give as much, if not a little more, than a previous visitor. Perhaps the need to be more mercenary than before altered the thinking of the Clan members and then brought them into the modern world, as they eventually became pacesetters, being the first people in Qufu to own a car.

The middle aged and older generations we met didn't seem to question the 'Party Line' but the younger people took full advantage of any small freedoms allowed. On Sundays, in some parks, informal 'English corners' sprang up where people, mostly young, went to practise their English skills and hoped that a foreigner might chance along. Whereas I was always happy to talk to people in the street, I avoided the English corners as I felt they were probably pretty closely watched by 'Them' to ensure none of the students got involved in any political discussion. I was happy to sit firmly 'on the fence' and not voice my own opinions about the politics of another country: after all, I could not know enough to give a fair comment. Undoubtedly some young people were becoming disenchanted with the expected blind acceptance of the 'rules' and although they attended (they had to) political meetings twice a week it was lip service only in many cases. They had caught a glimpse of what the West had to offer and were determined to get on the ladder of success, so they could have access to it all.

For every loosening of the reins there often seemed to be a clampdown, and these were given wide publicity in the newspaper, to discourage 'straying from the right path'. The reports ranged from the seizure and destruction of 'decadent music and printed matter' which someone was caught trying to import, to a train crash which killed 3 people and injured 147. Two track maintenance workers were held responsible and their negligence cost them 7 and 4 years in jail, and jail was not the humane institution we know. Even at its worst though, it could never have been as bad as the Mongolian Prison I once read about. Prisoners were incarcerated in wooden boxes the same shape as, and only slightly roomier than, coffins many of which were kept in one room. On one side of each box there was a small hole just large enough for a hand to pass through and once a day a warder gave food and drink to any prisoner who put his hand out. Once the box was closed it was never opened – the prisoner was never released – and if no hand appeared at mealtimes for three or four days then the box and its contents were buried. The showing of criminal trials on television and the graphic posters showing photos of victims and perpetrators did certainly act as something of a deterrent, as did capital punishment. Again things had progressed from the distant past when confessions were often extracted through torture, the most painful of which must surely have been the 'Death of a Thousand Cuts'. The 'victim's' body was encased in the equivalent of our chicken wire which was then tightened slightly until small pieces of flesh protruded through the holes. Razor sharp implements were then run over the body, slicing off the flesh down to the level of the wire. This process of very gently tightening and slicing slivers of raw flesh was repeated as often as necessary.

When I started teaching English with a joint venture company the classes were suddenly inundated with very eager students from a 'sister' organisation who were desperate to improve their language skills. The classes became unmanageably large, so I arranged to take the additional students on their own once a week, for which they would pay nothing. They made great progress for months, until suddenly I was told that the lessons had to stop because they were "too busy". It was obviously not the truth, but someone higher up the ladder had decided that close association with a foreigner was against the rules – despite the fact that nothing sensitive was ever mentioned and the classes were open to anyone who wished to check up on us.

During our seven years we saw a noticeable heightening of the standard of living and increase in wealth. The old 'wants' that everyone worked towards – bicycle, fridge, sewing machine and, latterly, television were fast attainable by virtually all and many people had begun to aim higher towards videos and freezers. Some of the better off families employed girls from the country as their ayis and quite a few men, desperate for money to afford the new 'luxuries' that were becoming available, 'moonlighted' by doing two jobs – including one taxi driver I encountered who worked in a factory at night and then came close to falling asleep at the wheel during the day. Perhaps the most 'up-market' show of affluence was the owning, by a few people, of a telephone pager (few private individuals even had telephones). Mind you, the Monopoly game I bought hadn't caught up, and the playing pieces were still Chinese wheelbarrows. Apart from possessions, travel began to come within the reach of more and more of the population. The seaside resort nearest to Beijing, Beidaihe, was used almost entirely in the early 80s by foreigners, high ranking cadres, Party officials and residents of the many sanitoria situated in the area. By 1986 nearly all the foreigners (except us!) holidayed in Thailand, the Philippines or Hawai'i, and Beidaihe was packed with Chinese people such as shop assistants and lift operators. Beijing itself also became a popular destination with Chinese families from the country.

In the countryside the increase in wealth was less obvious, and rural communities often had no electricity or running water to individual dwellings. Old wooden ploughs pulled by mules, stone threshing floors and mill wheels operated by 'donkey-power', threshers worked by men sitting on a bench pedalling treadles to turn the wood and metal machinery – these were the norm. One particular village we visited frequently made you feel you were stepping back in time, even though their main livelihood was quarrying marble and carving ornamental lions, gateways etc. which must have brought in a sizeable income to the area. Not a few of their carvings were exported (an ornamental gateway in Manchester's Chinatown was their work), but no sign of foreign influence or affluence seemed to have touched them, the majority of the intricate carving being done by hand. Farm animals wandered around the streets together with rosy-cheeked children. An incredibly old village bell hung from a rickety wooden scaffolding – anywhere else it would have been preserved in a museum. Purely selfishly I hoped it would not change, as life there seemed so natural and contented.

At one time farmers ('peasants' in Chinese) were very poor and so the government took active measures to increase their standard of living, to the extent that some young farmers were earning more than teachers or doctors for less work, which naturally gave rise to discontent amongst the 'white collar workers'. (The Chinese equivalent of that expression was 'collar cuff', managerial level being the only ones who normally wore shirts). On a visit to a rural area to the south of China we noticed that the majority of the farmers' single-storey houses had flat roofs, most unlike the normal style of architecture. It was explained to us that they were built thus so that as the owners saved more money they could easily add a second floor.

Despite the obvious and assumed differences between East and West, Them and Us, I found myself totally at home with all Chinese people I met and discovered that we basically all had the same hopes, fears, struggles and, perhaps most important of all, the same sense of humour. So saying, there were always little differences that amused or interested me.

Personal habits such as nose-blowing, nose-picking and staring didn't worry me, but the awful spitting took more coming to terms with. The polluted atmosphere (and presumably poor quality tobacco in many cases) did give rise to congestion and the need to 'clear the tubes' but the noise, rising deep from within to finish with a resounding plop, was enough to make the stoutest shudder. The worst was if you heard the awful noise behind you and wondered just where it would land, as spitting was done indiscriminately and you had to watch carefully where you stepped. If embarrassed, a Chinese person was likely to laugh, which could cause great misunderstanding, and not a little anger on the part of one particular tourist. A little boy was urinating and turned unexpectedly to view the foreigner he discovered standing nearby, thereby peeing all over the foreigner's feet. The mother, greatly embarrassed, laughed. A total stranger would ask you how old you were, but this originated from the etiquette of needing to show respect to one's elders rather than from nosiness. Similarly the often used greeting "where are you going?" was just a figure of speech and desired no more detailed, or true, answer than "walking" or "shopping".

If confronted by an accident or a stranger needing help a Chinese person would as likely as not stare, but make no attempt to help – 'don't get involved'. (There had at one time been a very old belief that if you aided someone whose house was on fire or flooded for example, then you would be robbing the dragon of fire, water, or whatever other disaster, of his prey and he would take his revenge on you instead). On the other hand, any opportunity to give unsolicited advice was never missed, whether it be on your clothing, health, children or purchases. Whilst browsing in a second-hand furniture shop Mike had found and bought a lovely wooden cupboard, which he returned to collect the following day. He parked as near as possible to the shop, but was slightly hampered by a wall of cabbages and a gutter full of slippery, rotting leaves. Carrying the large piece of furniture to the car immediately attracted a large crowd, all of whom offered advice as to the best way to squeeze it in. When the crowd eventually became too large, a policeman materialised from nowhere, moved them all on, and then stood and watched with an uninterrupted view of the proceedings. Slipping and sliding on the cabbage leaves, Mike eventually loaded it in, at which point an assistant arrived saying "what about the chairs?" It appeared that the cupboard was part of a set and came with two large chairs. They were far too nice to leave behind – and the crowd would never have allowed him to abandon something he'd paid for. The policeman had lost interest and had allowed a crowd to reassemble, who noisily suggested all manner of ways of fitting a quart into a pint pot. (It did eventually go in, more despite the advice than because of it!)

Chinese people were very genuine and very honest: you could safely leave your shopping, purse etc. unattended and hotel rooms never needed to be locked; but they did have one sometimes annoying habit of telling you what they *thought* you wanted to hear rather than the truth, lest they offend you. It could even happen in actions as well as words: realising that many tourists feared drinking tap water one hotel had a third tap fitted in all rooms, labelled 'drinking water'. An inquisitive engineer friend unscrewed the fascia board to discover it was just connected to the existing cold water tap. Guests drank it and their belief that it was especially treated kept them happy – and they didn't suffer any more or less than anyone else.

Loss of face was perhaps the most feared outcome of any confrontation between 'Them and Us', but could often be avoided. It was counterproductive to tell an ayi that she hadn't cleaned the windows properly, but to produce a brand new cloth and explain that it would make the job much easier than the hard work she'd had to put in last time… Sometimes a complete impasse seemed to be reached though: yak tails were exported to Britain for a part of ceremonial military dress but one shipment had fleas. One side demanded payment, the other replacement, and both swore the fleas weren't theirs. We left China before hearing the outcome of that particular argument, but privately joked that we expected any day a bill would arrive…'fleas are extra'!

Chapter Nine: Festivals, Superstitions and Symbolism

Our celebrations of Christmas and New Year gradually crept into Chinese life, but only to the extent of adopting a few of the traditions such as sending cards and decorating shops and hotels; the truly Chinese celebrations were still of far greater importance. The one we probably all know is Spring Festival (in the West often called Chinese New Year). My first experience of it was an ever more harassed Mrs. Yuan: prior to the turn of the year homes were given a total spring clean, and some even redecorated, after which preparations had to be made for the feasting. She was trying to buy and prepare around 40lbs each of meat and fish and masses of vegetables and fruit – and all without the convenience of fridge, freezer and convenience foods. Many goods were still rationed at that time and even if you saved up your coupons it was quite likely that the actual foodstuffs wouldn't be available anyway. Jiaozi were as much a part of Spring Festival as turkey is at Christmas, and families would get together around the table and all make them together. Multitudes of other delicious home-cooked dishes were expected too of course, including as many visually exotic items as possible, even down to steamed bread rolls shaped like very realistic hedgehogs. Large red apples could be purchased bearing the 'double happiness' symbol, ingeniously brought about by sticking a stencil over the apple as it ripened so that the character was paler than the rest of the skin. Even the day after the family celebrations there was no rest, as friends and associates would call uninvited, but unlike our 'first footing' a dram would not suffice and a fullblown meal was necessary.

Families tried wherever possible to be together for Spring Festival and there was a dramatic increase in the number of passengers on trains and buses and, latterly, planes. Presents such as we gave at Christmas were few, most children receiving new clothes, and visitors would give specially packaged and decorated cakes and sweets. The other absolute essential for the celebrations were fireworks, as noisy as possible, which were let off to scare away all evil spirits from the incoming year. As midnight approached a few rockets were set off to explode noisily overhead, but when the exact hour was reached it seemed that every house and flat in the entire city was letting off whole bundles of them simultaneously. The air was a mass of lights and explosions and the noise deafening. The amazing display continued unabated for a good half hour before gradually tailing off - hopefully without too many fires caused by wayward rockets landing on balconies overfull of stored boxes. Unfortunately many of the fireworks were far from safe and few people seemed to be aware of their inherent dangers. Vendors would display veritable barrages of rockets: one man I saw had carefully laid them out across the back of a flatbed three-wheeler bike but in such a way as they pointed horizontally across the pavement at waist height. As he sat waiting for customers he would occasionally lean over the fireworks to rearrange them, a lit cigarette hanging out of his mouth! Accidents caused by fireworks carried on trains led to their eventual ban and passengers' baggage was searched at all stations during the time leading up to the Spring Festival. Just to really hammer home the message, photographs of horrible burnt bodies, victims of a 'firework fire' on a train, were displayed at Beijing station.

There were many traditions and superstitions attached to Spring Festival: all outstanding debts had to be settled before the new year commenced, the family should have new clothes and, apart from jiaozi, special new year cake had to be eaten whose name *'nian gao'* also meant 'wealth in the coming year'. If the new year was 'your' animal of the twelve in the cycle, then at the stroke of midnight someone in your family had to tie a red sash around your waist, otherwise you risked a disastrous year ahead. Many of these traditions endured for years, but some of the older superstitions were retold for amusement rather than taken seriously: if you cried during the festival time you would want for food and clothes in the coming year, and you should not mention loss of money or sweep your home. If you bought a new pair of shoes at that time you might lose your voice and if you bathed immediately before gambling you'd have bad luck. Knives should not be used during the first few days of the new year to avoid cutting off good luck. Even if you avoided all those pitfalls you had to remember that on the 7th and 8th days the dragon raised his head and needles could not be used in case he was pricked in the eye.

Although it had become a purely secular occasion, in the past gods had featured in the Spring Festival. During the week prior to the day itself, pictures of vermilion-faced, fierce-looking gods were pasted on doors to frighten off evil spirits, and 'New Year Couplets' pasted either side of the doorways. The couplets, beautiful calligraphy on red paper, were to invoke success and happiness and sometimes reflected the occupation of the resident within: 'success in all ventures', 'may our customers be plentiful', 'bounteous harvest' or simply the hopes of the family: 'long life, many sons'. On some windows paper cuts appeared, these being very elaborate patterns, Chinese characters or animals, all intricately crafted by cutting out designs in sheets of thin paper. The artistry was best appreciated when you realised that they were all cut freehand, using tiny scissors, and without any sketched outline to follow. An old craft, they later expanded their scope to include large pictures depicting farming scenes, factories, jungles etc.

The god most associated with Spring Festival was the Kitchen God – no longer worshipped, but a story passed on from generation to generation. Seven or eight days prior to new year's day a picture of the god was put up in the house and sticky sweets placed before it. The belief was that after such 'sweetness' he would put in a good report about the family to the Jade Emperor in heaven, who in turn would bless them for the year. I had also heard another version that after eating the sticky sweets the Kitchen God's lips would be stuck together so he couldn't speak badly of you. The pictures would then be burnt to symbolise his return to heaven once more. As day broke on the first day of the new year, doors were opened to welcome the Kitchen God back and fresh pictures of him were pasted up, in the belief that blessings and domestic harmony accompanied his return.

Celebrations used to continue for more than the few days later allowed by a more commercial and business oriented society and the end of Spring Festival was marked, on the 15th day of the first lunar month, by the Lantern Festival. As always, traditional food had to be consumed, in this instance *'yuan xiao'*, small, almost suet pudding textured, boiled dumplings filled with a sweet sugary puree. The 15th day also being the first full moon, the festival was also linked with the welcoming of the brighter days of spring. In the streets vendors used to sell lanterns of all varieties ranging from simple decorated spheres to animals and even human shapes. Lit by oil or candle they would be displayed around houses and courtyards to be admired by all taking a stroll or passing by on their way to watch acrobatic or dance performances.

The only remaining vestiges that we encountered of the once celebrated Mid-Autumn or Moon Festival was the sale of moon cakes. No longer was the moon goddess worshipped, nor the bright new moon of autumn gazed upon, but the traditional food remained. Usually a sweet filling was encased in pastry, about the size of our pork pies, the top being beautifully decorated with designs of flowers, auspicious characters etc.

A more modern, and purely secular, annual celebration was National Day on October 1st, commemorating the founding of the Republic in 1949. Every large building in Beijing was permanently outlined with strings of light bulbs which were switched on for National Day (and some other festivals too). The effect was quite beautiful, especially as most of the buildings concerned had naturally ornate roofs with gently sloping lines. Tian An Men Square was the centre of celebration and large models were erected both there and at major crossroads. Wire mesh was fashioned into enormous dragons, phoenixes, pandas, elephants, models of the Great Wall, and during the last few days of September teams of people converged on the models and intertwined every inch of the mesh with greenery and flowers. Over the years the models became more and more complicated, some even being mechanised, and fountains and miniature gardens appeared in the Square. During the evening, as the lights were switched on and the models illuminated, hordes of people meandered down Chang An (which had all, instead of the usual half, of its street lights switched on for the special day), to congregate in Tian An Men, admire the decorations and take numerous photos. In one park in Qingdao, a city south east of Beijing, there was built an enormous dragon model, but instead of using greenery, empty green beer bottles from the local brewery were placed neck-first into the large wire mesh. The resulting 'bottle glass' effect of the bases of all the bottles gave the convincing look of a dragon's shiny scales.

During the late 80s there was a resurgence of a type of 'Temple Fair', the content and layout of which probably bore close resemblance to their age old predecessors. Held in parks around the city, whole avenues of stalls would be set up selling so many varieties of food that every conceivable taste must have been catered for, from savoury and spicy to kebab-like sticks of toffee-coated haw apples topped with a dragon or animal crafted in toffee. Having eaten you might feel the need to partake of a refreshing bowl of tea, but no mere teapot would do for such an occasion. Gigantic copper kettles about three feet high, with brass dragons undulating around the handle and spout were brought into use. The bottom section of the kettle was filled with charcoal to keep the tea warm, making the whole thing very heavy: I could scarcely lift an empty one, but such was the expertise of the, often elderly, vendors that they could lift one with one hand and pour a stream of hot tea into a small bowl without spilling a drop.

Other stalls sold clothes, small ornaments and toys, including two wonderful home-made ones. The first was sold around the time of the Lantern Festival and was a wood and wire frame about two feet long in the shape of a dog/lion. The 'skeleton' was covered in strips of finely cut, brightly coloured crepe paper, giving the overall effect of long fur. The head had piercing eyes made from half eggshells and the long floppy ears were so attached that they moved slightly as the dog was pulled along on little clay wheels. The whole head was mounted on a wooden pivot with a putty weight so that it nodded up and down. They were wonderful 'toys' designed as lanterns but I would never have risked putting a naked flame near all that paper: far more practical, if less artistic, were the newer inventions of hollow red plastic fish lanterns lit by two batteries and a small bulb. The second home-made toy for sale, and my all time favourite, appeared around Spring Festival and could best be described as a series of windmills. Small wheels made from thin bamboo strips with coloured tissue paper 'spokes' and a bamboo 'hub' were nailed onto bamboo frames. Simple combinations of cotton, paper and card were transformed into tiny drums and strikers which were then mounted behind each windmill. Waved in the air or, even better, mounted onto a bicycle, the breeze turned the wheels and each little drum clicked loudly. Most of the windmills had between three and five wheels but some gigantic creations boasted fifty. The colour of the paper spokes, the clicking drums and the delighted faces of both children and adults alike will always be synonymous with fairs and spring.

Having eaten and shopped you could then be entertained by the same performances that had been enjoyed for many generations. Stilt-walkers in brightly coloured costumes enacted traditional plays; women danced, waving long silk scarves which floated slowly in the air; muscled men balanced thick, heavy, flag-topped poles bigger than a caber, on their hands, feet, elbows and even chins and noses. The less strong sufficed with balancing mere chairs and tables! You could watch magic tricks worthy of the Magic Circle, and amazing female contortionists who could have made a fortune had they appeared on Western television. Fire-eaters, puppeteers, Chinese opera singers, performing birds – whatever your particular favourite you would find it at the fair.

All cultures have their age-old superstitions, often based on deep-felt beliefs but latterly only thought of as amusing stories: the Chinese ones I heard ranging from birth to death. In the days when it was all important to produce sons rather than daughters all manner of unusual ideas arose as to how to achieve it: a naked sword placed under the bridal mattress and the eating of peanuts and chestnuts was supposed to ensure male offspring. For every person you told that you were pregnant, an hour would be added to your labour, and if a man called unexpectedly during labour then the child born would be a boy. Should a baby son become ill, his parents would dress him as a girl so that the evil spirits would pass him by as being unworthy of their attention. One hundred days after birth, the baby's mouth should be rubbed with the head of a chicken, the tail of a fish and a crab, to make it easier to teach the child to eat.

Should you survive all that and grow to marriageable age, your wedding had certain superstitions attached: the bride, dressed in red (the lucky colour), arrived in a palanquin at the groom's house, whereupon firecrackers would be let off to scare away any evil spirits that might have followed her. The bride should be accompanied by a woman who was the mother of at least one living son. Round her neck the girl would wear a small mirror to prevent any malignant spirit entering her body (the spirits being so ugly they would be frightened off by their own reflections), and she had to cross the threshold with her left foot first. Later developments to the ceremony added feasting for three days, symbolic presents of a duck, a carp and a goose with its head painted red, and the poor bride being teased mercilessly by the groom's friends all remarking on her lack of beauty.

Should you have wished to hasten your death by committing suicide certain 'rites' had to be adhered to. Anyone of 'official' status would not terminate his life secretly, but would first bid farewell to his family and give instructions for the future. An unhappy servant girl or concubine's favoured way of suicide was to bang her head repeatedly against a wall (I would have thought it a rather difficult way to kill oneself), which would bring untold loss of face to her 'owners', who would try to hide the fact. It was not allowed for anyone except an Emperor, Empress or concubine to commit suicide inside the walls of Beijing – the common folk had to leave the city before ending their lives.

Once you were dead, of course, you didn't have to worry about the superstitions of this life, but not so those left behind. Each period of mourning lasted for seven days, the first five such periods (i.e. thirty five days) being 'deep mourning' when white had to be worn. Thereafter was 'secondary mourning' when violet or blue was worn on the anniversary of the death. The funeral itself carried certain codes of dress, such as coloured strips of cloth attached to the heels of the white shoe coverings worn by the chief mourners. The different colours denoted the relationship to the deceased. If the dead person had been of high standing, the coffin was carried around the streets followed by a long procession, and on the coffin was sometimes placed a bowl of water. This was to demonstrate the care and respect of the pall bearers that, despite a long journey along uneven streets, not a drop of water was spilt.

We all have numbers that we think of as lucky or unlucky and numbers featured often in Chinese symbolism. The number four was considered unlucky as in Chinese it sounded similar to the word for death. Nine, on the other hand, was the most auspicious of all, being the highest single number, and was often associated with the Emperor. All the doors of the Imperial palaces were adorned with nine rows of nine gold coloured studs, and the Forbidden City had a total of nine thousand nine hundred and ninety nine rooms (and a half, some said), only heaven itself having more, with ten thousand. The other number that featured frequently was twelve, and fortunes, or misfortunes such as earthquakes and floods, were thought to recur every twelve years. There was a story that Buddha once invited all the animals to visit him one new year's day, but only twelve of them turned up, so to thank them they not only each had a year named after them but ruled for that year. Today the twelve year cycle still features the horse, sheep, monkey, rooster, dog, pig, rat, ox, tiger, rabbit, dragon and snake (sometimes called 'little dragon').

Probably the most commonly seen symbol in China was that of the dragon, whose history dated back to the original totem of the ancient Xia tribe, which was a snake. After they had conquered other tribes, they incorporated their totems with their own, the new ones including animals, birds, fish and reptiles. The eventual outcome was the dragon, which incorporated parts of nine (what else!) animals: the horns of a deer, the head of a camel, the eyes of a rabbit, the skull of a snake, the stomach of a clam, the scales of a fish, the five claws of an eagle, the paws of a tiger and the ears of an ox. On its back it had eighty one (nine times nine) scales; its breath could turn into water or fire; it could change its size or become invisible and was believed by some to be deaf. The dragon was also representative of the Emperor's authority, the Emperor being called

'The Heavenly Son of the True Dragon'. The Imperial face was referred to as 'The Dragon Visage'; anyone said to be a 'hidden dragon' was considered as a potential Emperor. Only the Emperor ever wore or used the colour yellow, so dragons were often painted that colour too.

The great dragon had nine sons, all with differing qualities and depicted in different places:
Haoxian was reckless and adventurous and found on the eaves of palaces.
Yazi was valiant and bellicose and found on sword and knife hilts.
Chiwen gazed into the distance and was found on roof beams.
Baxia was a good swimmer and was found on bridges and piers.
Pulao was fond of roaring and was found on bells.
Bixi was an excellent pack animal and was found on supports.
Qiuniu loved music and was found on instruments.
Suanmi was fond of smoke and fire and was found on incense burners.
Jiaotu was tight-lipped and was found on doors.

Chapter Ten: Visitors

Whenever an important visitor, be it royalty, dictator, head of state etc. visited the capital his or her imminent arrival was 'announced' by the hanging of large strings of silk flags of assorted colours at regular intervals across Chang An, starting at the junction with the airport road and ending at the turn off for the State Guest House. The accommodation there was in fact not in one house but in a complex of houses, each having enough room for the VIP and the accompanying entourage, with private dining and sitting rooms. These houses were set in wonderful gardens abounding in flowers, and tree-surrounded lakes with very 'Chinese-style' bridges. The site was originally a favourite Imperial fishing lake – hence its name Diaoyutai or Fishing Platform. In Tian An Men Square each lamp standard bore two flags: the Chinese one and that of the country of the guest. From our flat, overlooking the main thoroughfare, we could always tell when the cavalcade of official cars was nearby, by the sound of police sirens, and within minutes all other traffic was stopped, or pushed off the road, as the police cars and hongqis sped past at breakneck speed. I would have thought it better to allow the visitor to see more on his journey and less risk of killing a few cyclists en route, but the responsibility for the foreigner's safety didn't allow for that. The drivers of these 'cavalcade' cars were highly skilled: driving close enough to the car in front so as not to allow any 'outside' vehicle to cut in, but should there be a need to brake quickly, the second, fourth and every alternate car throughout the line would steer promptly to the left thus giving all the cars additional stopping distance.

On two occasions the flags flying in the Square were Union Jacks: first for Mrs. Thatcher and the second time for the Queen. Mrs. Thatcher's visit entailed a good deal of work and organisation by the Embassy, but neither Mike nor I had any significant role to play, being in the enviable position of enjoying the receptions and social events free of any responsibility for their smooth running. Mike attended a reception at the Ambassador's residence and had the opportunity to talk to Mrs. Thatcher about possible Naval liaison and business, but found it somewhat difficult to hold a lucid conversation as a news reporter was actually standing on his foot in his efforts to eavesdrop! That evening, while Mrs. Thatcher attended yet another reception, Denis was to enjoy a quiet few hours at the flat of the Defence Attaché. While Mike wasn't involved in either occasion, he was detailed off to escort Denis to the Colonel's home. The temperamental lift decided to have one of its many 'off' days and unceremoniously deposited the two of them in the basement rather than ascending to floor 15. It was obliging enough to open its doors, but far from keen to close them again, so there they stood gazing out onto stark dusty concrete and the occasional cockroach (the rats must have been elsewhere). Once you had explained (whilst wrestling with the door mechanism) that in theory all the basements were linked to a vast network of tunnels enabling all the residents of the city to evacuate to the country in the event of nuclear attack, there was little small talk left. Fortunately by that time the lift decided it'd had its little joke and suddenly closed its doors and headed for the fifteenth floor.

A few evenings after her visit we received videos of British television news footage: it was always fascinating to see events reported that you were familiar with and to see the different slants put on them by different reporters. The particular footage on the tape showed Mrs. Thatcher's stumble on the steps of the Great Hall of the People and all sorts of speculation that she was overtired, overworked, ill or even on the verge of a complete breakdown! If only the reporters had had the time to investigate further, and ask any one of us who had had to negotiate those particular steps many times, they would have discovered that nearly everyone got the 'vertigo' effect on the descent, but we had learnt the slalom technique so that you were never looking directly down the long white expanse.

I don't know how many months of planning went in to the Royal visit, but I suspect it was many, and for that event Mike was heavily involved, for the Royal Yacht came too. His first task was to answer an official query from the Chinese hosts: "Will the Queen be bringing the Royal Yacht with her on the plane?" He moved 'operations' to Shanghai

(Britannia's first port of call) six days before the Queen's arrival in China, leaving me to enjoy the excitement in Beijing. As I suspect with all such great events, things do go wrong behind the scenes but are never obvious to the visitors or observers. Upon their arrival at the airport the Queen and Prince Philip were to be driven directly to the Residence for a welcome reception. Last minute details were all under control when a couple of Iranians upset the applecart by being discovered wandering around the garden. Their intentions were in fact totally innocent: they were looking for the visa section and had entered the Residence by mistake (the gates were all but identical). That potential problem solved, the guests were all mustered into their places and the children lined up clutching their flags, and there was still ten minutes to go. Communications were constantly checked between the cavalcade driving from the airport and the liaison staff in the garden. A casual enquiry from the Residence garden of "Where are you now?" elicited the reply "Just passing a large building with C-I-T-I-C on the roof – does that mean anything to you?" Did it mean anything! It meant that they were a lot closer than we'd expected, and the Ambassador was still chatting with guests at the far end of the lawn. A sprightly member of the staff was despatched who, reportedly, politely interrupted the conversation with an "Excuse me, sir, RUN."

The rest of the event passed without a hitch – well on the surface anyway. Those who were fortunate enough to be presented to Her Majesty were lined up inside, when the Embassy nurse was called away from the line to attend to an elderly expat who was taken ill. The problem was no more serious than a reaction to standing too long and an unaccustomed glass of champagne, and once he was reassured and sat down, the nurse was able to just make it back to her place in time. I had always admired Royalty for their ability to find something to say to everyone they met; in my case we discussed the Yacht, its progress and arrival in Shanghai and the position of the threatened typhoon in the Canton area. Fortunately when the children were approached, Jonathan had remained smiling, but silent. One of the things we had brought with us to China was an electric train set which Mike had promised to set up 'after the Queen's visit'. I had harboured visions of his asking her "When are you going home, because then my dad can do my train set."

The evening of the Queen's arrival saw us at a superb banquet at the Great Hall of the People – a wonderful repast with a cleverly selected menu of dishes easier than most to manage with chopsticks for those not accustomed to their frequent use. Fortunately no water melon – I was reminded of a banquet I attended where I could see the dilemma of Chinese guests: what do you do to politely extract the myriad seeds you inevitably end up with in your mouth. Being an 'old hand' at 'ways Chinese' I unashamedly spat mine out onto my plate – to the horror of the Western guests and the relief and delight of the Chinese ones, who followed suit.

After the meal, and the speeches, there was to be a 'soirée' in the Great Hall's auditorium, to which we repaired after the necessary pause for the toilets. Naturally we could not leave the dining area until all the top guests and VIPs had done so, so by the time table number 12 was allowed out, there was little time before the performance was to begin. Two of us rushed off to the ladies – quite a distance – and then hurried in the direction of the theatre, but just ahead of us we suddenly saw the Queen and her attending party leaving a side room. Should we have continued, our paths would have crossed, yet if we had held back and followed after the Royal party we would have been late taking our seats or even refused admission. Something must have flashed through my mind on Imperial etiquette – you must never turn your back on the Emperor, so presumably the same applied here. Without even pausing to think of the more modern protocol involved, I heard myself whispering to the lady at my side, "Walk backwards as fast as you can, but try to look as if you're really walking forwards." Somehow no one noticed our antics, we reached a secondary staircase and, once out of sight, descended two at a time and arrived breathlessly in our seats.

What stamina – receptions, banquets, speeches etc. and then a cultural performance, and throughout it all the Queen managed to remain alert, interested and awake – which was more than could be said of some of the audience seated around me, who were dozing happily. The whole evening was running late and some of the 'acts' had to be cut, which was a shame, although I personally could have lived without the rather long excerpt from Much Ado About Nothing translated into Chinese and sung in the style of Peking Opera. It might have been more entertaining were I more familiar with the original play I suppose. Finally the Royal party were invited onto the stage to meet members of the cast and the Queen was presented not with a bouquet of flowers but with a basket of them – the biggest one I had ever seen, being about the size of a desk and needing two people to carry it. When placed at her feet she was obliterated from the chest down – if size of bouquet were any indication of esteem, then they were more than delighted by her attendance that night.

Judging by the Chinese TV news, the visit to Shanghai went equally well. Enormous numbers of people turned out on the streets to see the Royal visitors, although I suspected that the reporters might have been a little misled: all the streets were closed to all but official vehicles and it was the afternoon rush hour. That, combined with the Chinese love of staring, gave film footage of hordes of waiting people – but quite a few were undoubtedly just waiting for the roads to open so they could go home. Even in Beijing there had been some confusion as to the identity of the visitor: more than one man in the street when asked who the Queen of England was replied "Mrs. Thatcher". Nor did all stories reach the media. There was an unsubstantiated one circulating of houses being demolished simply to improve the width and aspect of a certain street to be used by the cavalcade, and a true one telling of the problems of the Royal Standard. That particular flag was only flown when the Queen was present and had to break (fly free) at the exact moment of her arrival. The flagpole in the Consul General's garden in Shanghai was in a flowerbed which had unfortunately been thickly planted with particularly thorny rose bushes. Mike enquired as to whether it might be possible to raise the Standard just before her arrival. "No", came the reply. "She notices such things." So be it. The Queen's arrival found Mike standing in the midst of the roses ready to pull the right rope at the right time. The

Standard fluttered in the breeze just when meant to and, judging by conversations later in the day, she does notice such things as Naval Attachés in rose bushes!

Some of us flew to Canton for the unique opportunity to attend a reception on board the Royal Yacht – and we were very impressed: never had I seen such gleaming brass, such shining wooden decks. Mike had been on the Yacht for some time and was lined up with various other Officers to escort guests away from the receiving line and into the salon where drinks were served. Seeing me approaching, he turned to the Officer next to him and said in a low voice "I fancy the blonde in the red dress. I'll take that one, and I bet you anything you like I spend the evening with her." Shocked by such uncouth behaviour, his companion was speechless as Mike approached me and, showing no sign of recognition, held me by the arm and led me away. Someone obviously eventually put the poor Officer out of his misery at such un-officer-like behaviour, as when I met him towards the end of the evening he smiled, winked and said "Good evening, *Mrs. Farr.*"

I had seen and heard the Band of the Royal Marines perform Beat The Retreat only on television and that had been moving enough, but nothing could ever compare with the emotions stirred by seeing and hearing them on the jetty at Canton, whilst standing on the deck of HMS Britannia. Filled with great feelings of patriotic pride we finally left the Yacht to stand on the jetty and watch the Chinese performers entertain the Queen immediately prior to her departure – hopefully to avoid the still threatening typhoon. The performance was carefully timed to finish at exactly the moment when the Yacht sailed, so it had been drummed into the organisers that it was imperative they start on time. They did that, but unfortunately none of the Royal party had arrived on deck at that point. They did get to see most of the wonderful 'Lion Dance' but, appreciative of its beauty, a message was sent asking if it could be started over again. Disaster was averted through Mike's impassioned pleas that once the meticulously rehearsed and rigidly timed performance had started it would result in complete pandemonium to try to stop it and regroup to begin again – tantamount to stopping an avalanche.

When ships leave jetties there always seems a great deal of activity of letting go lines, passing commands etc. but with the Royal Yacht it was such a well practised, smooth and silent affair that none of us noticed until the performance was over that she was already some yards from the quay. The only noticeable movement was a glimpse of something white being thrown from the rails to the shore – but it turned out to be Mike's white uniform jacket which he had left on board. Everyone involved was highly delighted with the success of the visit – no less the Chinese hosts and those dealing with the more practical aspects of the whole affair. Just as we were leaving, Mike heard his name being called and the Secretary of the Harbour Board Communist Party approached and threw his arms around Mike's shoulders in a mutual 'thank goodness it all went according to plan'.

As we sat in the coffee shop of the White Swan Hotel in Canton, Mike told me some of the things that very nearly didn't go according to plan! Britannia prided herself on always arriving at exactly the prearranged time, quite literally to within a minute. This had been duly relayed to the Canton harbour administrators, who then gave Mike a lecture on ships not being taxis. As it turned out the pilot vessel was anxious to get home early and led the Yacht at a cracking pace, forcing it to arrive – EARLY! (Mike's hotel was some 2 hours' drive away through very heavy traffic, so he only just made it himself.) With the help of the young and enthusiastic hotel business centre manager, communications were established between Mike and the Yacht, but this had also led to a few misunderstandings. When the telex came through from Royal Yacht Britannia they were asked if they wanted to book a room, and after messages had been relayed etc. the hotel very politely signed off with 'Goodnight, Mr. Britannia.' Probably the most potentially problematic hitch (apart from the alarmingly last minute clearing of the rubbish from the jetty) was the checking of passports. The number produced for inspection did not tally with the number of visitors and demands were made to see the passport of one H.M. Queen. It was very hard to explain to a Chinese official that it was possible for anyone not to have a passport yet still be allowed to travel abroad. None of the arguments Mike could think of seemed to help until he finally said "But your leader, Deng Xiaoping, doesn't have a passport." He almost certainly does, but enough doubt had been put into the official's mind to persuade him to allow the Queen to continue her journey without one.

Not all VIPs were of such high standing, but were nevertheless much welcomed by the Embassy, and their visits much enjoyed. There was great excitement amongst the younger people when news broke of the visit to Beijing of the Watford Football Team and their manager Elton John. A meeting was convened to decide how best to entertain them when not involved in matches, and it was finally decided that as they were young men rather than middle-aged diplomats, and as their Chinese hosts would hold a banquet or reception for them, that they might prefer a less formal, more relaxed evening with us with a buffet supper and a disco. There being insufficient room in the Residence it was to be held in the Amenities Hall, giving plenty of space to chat and drink at the bar or to dance. With the numbers involved it would have been astronomically expensive to have outside catering, so the wives provided the buffet: those with cooks providing salads (only cooks could find anything worth eating in that line), we all made puddings etc. and I arranged, through a contact, to have 100 fresh rolls specially made by the air catering bakery and to have 5 iceberg lettuces flown in from Hong Kong. Meat posed a bit of a problem – ham being the only edible offering locally – so we all agreed to relinquish the frozen turkeys we had earmarked for the following Christmas, in the hope that we could replace them.

On the night, the buffet seemed sumptuous, to us at any rate, the disco was certainly lively and everyone appeared to have a really good evening, to the extent that the team begged their coach driver to postpone the return trip to their hotel until the early hours of the morning. In view of that, we were very saddened to hear, a few days after, of an article in the British Press criticising the Embassy for their treatment of Watford Football Team. Apparently the person interviewed said they'd expected a formal reception in the Residence hosted by the Ambassador and were instead given a cold, self-service supper in the equivalent of a church hall. The whole thing was rather hurtful, primarily because we were given no opportunity to put our side of the story: the Ambassador had other official functions once or twice a day throughout the team's stay, the Hall was the best we had to offer (and a lot better than many Embassies could boast) and we genuinely believed they'd enjoy that kind of evening. Hopefully that report represented a minority view and the others did enjoy themselves – whatever, we did our best and we enjoyed the disco!

Naval visitors naturally involved Mike completely and on several occasions I was able to 'tag along' on visits both within the capital and further afield. I thoroughly enjoyed all these tours: there's nothing quite like showing a country you love to a newcomer to it, and I often found myself working alongside the Guide/interpreter and adding anecdotes. The visitors always seemed to enjoy themselves too, but the one visit that will probably always carry the fondest memories for me was that of the then First Sea Lord, Admiral Sir William Staveley and his wonderful wife, Bettina. They don't come any higher in the Navy, so we were rather apprehensive should things go wrong, but once we had met them we soon realised that they would have taken any situation calmly and with a large dose of good humour. Less relaxed was the wife of the chief Chinese host: she'd never been involved in that kind of thing before and was extremely nervous, and she not only had to entertain Lady Staveley in Beijing, but accompany her on a tour of the unknown to her cities of Tianjin, Xi'an, Shanghai, Zhanjiang, Guangzhou and Shenzhen. For the hectic Beijing part of the tour Mike and I moved into the State Guest House with them and from there several pleasant days were spent visiting the usual sights such as the Great Wall, Ming Tombs, Temple of Heaven, Forbidden City etc. although we did manage to steer the organisers away from the idea of taking our guests to Kentucky Fried Chicken for lunch, even if they were proud of that new addition to the famous sights of the city. The offer of paying thirty pounds to stand on the very spot on the gateway from where Chairman Mao announced the Republic was also declined in favour of a walk around Tian An Men Square and a try at kite flying with the help of an old man who was obviously a bit of an expert. The 'walkabout' attitude was totally foreign to the Chinese way of organising visitors, but they adapted very fast and as we stood in the square we were soon surrounded at a discreet but measured distance by a ring of bodyguards all facing outwards, and our official cars were quickly moved so as to be close at hand if needed. Whilst in Beijing we were all invited to Navy Headquarters, where we all sat drinking tea while the Admirals talked, one of the main topics of conversation being how highly the Chinese Navy thought of Mike and what a great bridge he was between the two Navies: it was extremely flattering and very embarrassing, but Sir William saw the funny side of it and believed it when we said we had nothing to do with it! Following the discussions we moved outside to view a march-past of the smartest sailors anyone could ever hope for, all in perfect straight lines, in perfect step and equally matched for height. Comparing notes afterwards both Mike and I admitted that our hearts swelled with pride and we were proud of 'our lads' – only we suddenly realised that they weren't 'ours'. We felt so at home in China that it was as if they were. That feeling was brought home to me even more at one of the banquets. It was customary at some time during the meal for the chief host to leave his table and, taking his glass with him, to toast each of the guests at the other tables. When it came to our group, the host touched glasses with every guest except me. There was great embarrassment amongst the other hosts, and he was quietly told of his error. "Oh, no – she is more host than guest now" was his reply. I had seldom felt prouder.

Our first foray outside was to Tianjin, a relatively short drive away, including a pit-stop where the toilets had obviously been completely spring-cleaned for our use. The city was very interesting, but regrettably the request to visit the old site of the Taku Forts had to be refused. The next leg of the tour was to Xi'an, principally to see the amazing excavations of the terracotta army, where the security arrangements for the statues had been greatly increased following the successful theft of one of the heads. The thief was caught when he tried to sell the piece of sculpture: for which he forfeited his own head. Better by far to buy one of the replicas being mass-produced by the locals and sold in the markets.

The time spent in Shanghai coincided with the Lantern Festival, giving a chance to view a marvellous exhibition of silk lanterns. They varied in size from small to enormous, and not all were really lanterns, but models of characters from literature and history. There were models of goddesses sitting in lotus flowers, the petals of which moved gently by means of a small motor, and life-sized scenes from the classic 'The Water Margin'.

The plane taking us from Shanghai to Guangzhou was delayed, but not for us the frustrations of sitting around at the airport, albeit in the VIP lounge. We spent the hours relaxing, chatting over cups of tea and coffee at the city's Guest House until the call came through summoning us to the plane. One handy tip I picked up on that trip was a way to identify your own suitcases: you tied a short length of coloured ribbon to the handle – it made for instant identification. The hotel in Guangzhou seemed to feed us up with an enormous breakfast, to be followed in the evening by a large banquet. After such a gastronomic day we felt in need of a walk before bed – much to the consternation of our Chinese 'minders'. Only slightly happier to be told that only Lady Staveley would go out with us, and unable to actually stop us, we headed off like children playing truant. Upon our return we noticed two of our 'minders' taking a stroll on the pavement outside the hotel – despite their casual remarks about its being a nice night for a walk, we all knew full well that they'd been unable to relax until we were safely back.

Shenzhen was a 'Special Economic Zone', giving it certain favourable taxation and trading rights, and was supposed to be China's answer to Hong Kong. We were shown around various export exhibitions displaying a wide variety of goods from cassette players to gold disco-wigs, and one particularly novel dance floor. It was square and marked out into smaller squares, but it was not for its appearance that we were summoned to view it. A glamorously dressed dancer appeared, and as her feet touched the different areas of the floor so a different note sounded – and it was no simple, slow tune she literally tapped out.

It was from Shenzhen that our guests left China, being met at the border and driven in to Hong Kong. Obviously few, if any, VIPs left that way, as there were no lounges etc. and we stood by the side of the road beside some lorries. It had been a wonderful tour, they had proved to be perfect guests, and the Chinese host's wife who had been so anxious, had relaxed totally after a couple of days, and as the Staveleys waved goodbye and drove off she had tears in her eyes to see them go.

One of the most rewarding of Naval visits must have been the unique series of lecture tours at the Submarine Academy in Qingdao. This port had been a German concession, the effects of which could still be seen clearly in the architecture and the pale, Germanic, delicious and renowned Qingdao beer. Mike had previously spent time at the Academy lecturing to Chinese Submarine Officers and it had been such a success that arrangements had been made for it to be an annual event. His visit had been the first – as someone pointed out to him when he arrived. "If you'd walked through those gates a few years ago we'd probably have shot you." On the occasion of his first lecture it looked as if they had: the floor of the lecturer's podium had been specially repainted in red but not enough time had elapsed for it to dry out. As he sat at the desk he was aware that his shoes were beginning to stick to the floor and when he left the lecture room a line of blood-red footprints followed behind. There were two further lecture visits after that and although we didn't attend for the whole time, we made a point of visiting for a couple of days to iron out any problems. The first couple, Richard and Eve Compton-Hall, lectured valiantly despite long hours, a draughty hotel dining room with several broken windows, and repetitive food. The kitchen seemed to serve up the same food at every meal and even the most ardent lover of Chinese food sometimes longed for a change – in this case an omelette was the dream. Noticing that 'eggs with tomato' was on the menu, I enquired as to why it could not be served: the message from the kitchen was that it was 'meiyou' because there were no tomatoes. Amidst great suckings of teeth and remarks that it would never taste as good, they agreed to serve us just the eggs – and quite delicious they were too. The third series of lectures, specialising in helicopter operations, was undertaken by two younger Naval Officers: an equally successful time was passed in Qingdao, their one frustration during their time in China being not the food but the playing of the same Richard Clayderman tape in every hotel restaurant and foyer in every city they visited on their meandering trip to Canton.

For a few years we were frequently called upon to assist defence sales delegations – at a time when trade seemed to be opening up between Britain and China. We always had a thoroughly enjoyable time with these hardworking teams, who often suffered many frustrations in their paths to the signing (or not!) of contracts, not to mention the maotai which flowed with the speed and ferocity of the Yangtse River in full flood. I well remember searching the lounges, toilets and rainsoaked muddy gardens of one restaurant for a delegation member who had left the table slightly the worse for wear, and then disappeared. Only some hours later did we, the mud-spattered and none too sober search party, discover that he had found himself a taxi and headed back to the hotel. In the first years of delegation visits the standard of accommodation available left a lot to be desired and one particular team rejoiced when they finally achieved not a contract but toast and strained orange juice for breakfast. It had been necessary for one of the party to go into the kitchen and teach them how to do it.

All delegations seemed to really appreciate a good, recognisable, Western meal at our flat to break the round of banquets; as one of their number put it, "to eat food that you can recognise and not be told at 8.30 that you must be tired." Oh the temptation to say "No. Not tired in the least." Undoubtedly the most welcome meal we provided was to a delegation who found themselves in Beijing for Christmas. They had all been due to return home long before, but negotiations had dragged on and on and they didn't dare risk losing the deal by disappearing off to the U.K. for a couple of weeks. Their employers went to great lengths to ensure their families had as good a time as possible over the festive season, but there was little they could do for those stranded at the other side of the world, so we determined to give them a Christmas lunch they'd never forget. We overfed them, and ourselves, on every traditional morsel we could lay our hands on: turkey, sausagemeat, stuffing, bacon, bread sauce, gravy, cranberry sauce, mashed and roasted potatoes and cauliflower (a local one with the rotten bits removed). Shame about the brussels sprouts, but you can't have everything – as it was, we had more variety than we'd normally ever have indulged in. As if that weren't enough we finished off with flaming Christmas pudding, brandy butter, cream and mince pies – all washed down with champagne brought by the guests. Not because of the amount of food, but because of the company and the feeling of being like fellow castaways, we felt it was the best Christmas meal we'd ever had.

It was three in the afternoon by the time we had to admit defeat, decline any more 'second helpings' and stagger to the sitting room for coffee. A knock at the door heralded not carol singers but the delivery of invitations to a banquet at the Great Hall of the People in a mere three hours' time! Some tried walking, others a shower, others the washing up – anything to put our digestive systems into gear for a second large meal. Our hosts had really pulled the stops out for the delegation as they'd realised that they'd given up on a very special celebration to stay in Beijing. Their major regret apart from that was that despite scouring both town and countryside, they had failed to find traditional turkey for us – and weren't we relieved! What they did serve us was the best selection of fish and seafood that I had ever tasted – oh to be less full, or in a culture that encouraged the use of doggy bags.

Accompanying delegations out of the city was always enjoyable, although things didn't always go smoothly. Mike escorted a group from the Royal College of Defence Studies, and halfway through the flight from Beijing to Shanghai the Brigadier sitting next to him suddenly started to look distinctly uncomfortable. After a few minutes he gave a groan and half stood up, pulling off his seatbelt, before collapsing into the aisle. One of the party was, fortunately, a Surgeon Captain, who took charge of the 'patient', but by that time the plane was in an uproar as the Chinese passengers all stood and pushed to get a better view. The co-pilot arrived and asked Mike if the casualty was dead: on learning that he wasn't he suggested keeping him warm, causing an avalanche of blankets proffered by helpful passengers. The engineer then arrived from the cockpit dragging a cylinder of oxygen – that was declined by the Surgeon Captain, leaving Mike to hold both oxygen and scores of blankets. By that time the poor Brigadier was showing some signs of life and started to make guttural, retching noises – immediately Mike was further deluged, that time by sick bags. The captain of the aircraft was the next person to arrive on the scene (the co-pilot having returned to the controls) – he had come to assess the situation for himself and announced that their landing in Shanghai would be an emergency one. He reluctantly agreed that the casualty be allowed to remain in the aisle for the landing, but only on the condition that his seat be occupied by a stewardess (quite why, no one seemed sure). After screeching to a halt on the runway the passengers were ushered off either end of the plane to avoid actually treading on the poor man, their departure being immediately followed by the arrival on board of two doctors/ambulancemen wearing white coats that would not have seemed out of place after a day's work at an abattoir! The Brigadier was recovering fast and Mike had to explain to these new arrivals that their help really wasn't needed – to avoid loss of face he explained that the Surgeon Captain was a most eminent British doctor: had he been any less eminent then their services would have been most welcome, even essential. That the right decision had undoubtedly been made was reinforced by the view of the dirty, tatty old van with a shakily hand-painted red cross on the side, together with an ancient stretcher that had probably seen good service in the Crimean War. (The Brigadier recovered within 24 hours and continued with the tour none the worse for the experience).

Visitors concerned with business ventures were dealt with by the Embassy's Commercial Section; those involved in the arts, by the Cultural Section and those of a military nature, by the Defence Section, but where did policemen, firemen and mountaineers fit in? Someone's obscure thinking deposited them at the door of the Naval Attaché – for which we were very grateful, for they were fascinating and entertaining guests. Chris Bonnington delighted us all by showing slides of a recent expedition. Breathtaking is a rather inadequate word to describe what he showed us and we were enthralled by his stories so graphically told that we could almost feel, as he had done, the air literally alive with electricity as lightning struck all around. After his talk we invited him to join us for a meal at the Jianguo Hotel, together with the Nepalese Military Attaché and his beautiful wife. The latter invitation turned out to be pure inspiration: over the large salad starter (which, as all mountaineers I'd met, Chris demolished as if it were a mere taster) it unfolded that he was encountering one particular stumbling block in his mountaineering arrangements with the authorities. Smiling at the name mentioned, our Nepalese friend revealed that the person was an old friend of his, to whom he would write that very night. I never found out if the problem was overcome, but if it was, and if we'd had any small part to play in it, then it might have in some way repaid the pleasure Chris's talk had given us.

When Mike invited one mountaineering team to dinner at our flat he stressed to them that the dress code was very, very casual as we knew they would only have their basic kit with them. Imagine our horror when we answered the knock at the door and were met by a stunning American girl in a designer little black dress. Our mouths must have gaped open, and we were very aware of our deliberately tatty jeans. Suddenly laughter broke out as the others came out of hiding – as informally dressed as we'd expected. The girl had had her father send out the dress to meet her upon her arrival in Beijing in case of an invitation to a smart dinner. Fortunately I'd anticipated the mountaineering appetite and had doubled the quantity of all the food – and it still nearly all disappeared. My usual pièce de résistance for pudding was home-made ice cream, but I wasn't sure how it would be received as the team had spent some considerable time holed up in the snow and I imagined that anything vaguely reminiscent of that wouldn't be popular. How wrong could you get – to my amazement several of them had passed some of the time dreaming about the food they'd eat once they were off the mountain, and ice cream had featured high on the list of favourites. We spent a wonderful evening with them, listening to anecdotes such as the 'mountaineers' book'. Cut off from a large proportion of their belongings, they discovered that they did have one paperback book between them and to avoid long waits for a turn of it, the first 'reader' would tear out each page as he'd finished it and pass it on to reader number two, and so on. Then there was the lady with the wooden leg! She wasn't anything to do with the climb, but in the rather confused reports coming in from the snowbound area, this tourist with a wooden leg kept being mentioned.

The more people who wanted permission to climb mountains in China, the more difficult, both financially and bureaucratically, it seemed to become. One team, having already paid an exorbitantly high price to climb and to hire porters etc. then wanted to store a few things in a small barn before starting on the final leg of the ascent. For the use of this dilapidated old shack they were charged the equivalent of a suite of rooms in the Beijing Hotel! They had also wanted to hire a yak, but were told they would have to buy one. This they did, but after a short time the emaciated old beast died and, having paid dearly for it and not wanting to waste their money, they decided to eat it. "Oh no", they were told, "you can't eat it. What you bought was a pack animal, not a meat animal. Meat animals are more expensive and if you want to eat this one then you must pay the difference." Nor was it just the mountaineers who were asked for outlandish payments. The film crew trying to shoot at the Great Wall were at their wits' end at the number of curious locals who wandered into every shot, in their curiosity to see what was going on, and the director made a series of ever more impassioned pleas to the Chinese coordinator to keep them out of the way. After several hours of total frustration and wasted footage the director finally admitted defeat. "Okay, let them stay. They can be part of the crowd scene", to which came the reply "Oh. You want 'extras' now. You'll have to pay for them you know."

As China became more 'open' so more and more individual visitors, groups and delegations flocked in, to the extent that the Embassy had no knowledge of many of them and opportunities were often missed to offer a welcome at the least, support if necessary or, at times, a chance to see beyond the tourist view to the 'real' China beneath. An article in a British newspaper was the first we knew about the proposed London to Beijing Car Rally, and it took some investigation on our part to find out the date of arrival in the city. 'Rally' conjured up fast cars and checkpoints, but what we saw arriving was more of a wondrous expedition consisting of all manner of vehicles from vintage to modern, and even a motorbike and sidecar. The distance travelled each day was geared to the slowest vehicle's capabilities, there was no element of competition, hotels had been booked ahead, time was allowed for some sightseeing and a full support team of mechanics accompanied them. That's my kind of rally. At the reception we hosted for them one evening, we heard of a few of the crises they had encountered, some of which happened before they had even left British shores. One couple had prepared for many months for the event and set out on the appointed day in their brand new, specially fitted-out four wheel drive vehicle – only to break down in a very big way before they'd even reached the rendezvous point at Marble Arch. Determined not to miss out on the journey of a lifetime they got towed home, transferred their kit to the family runabout and headed for China – and made it without a single hitch. Nor were we ever to make derogatory remarks about Lada cars again: a Lada was amongst the cars to make it all the way without needing any more attention than refuelling.

For some visitors we were quite pleased to have no prior warning: one couple turned up demanding to see the Ambassador, but were eventually persuaded to see a lesser mortal. They had arrived by train and were appalled at the crowds, the lack of queuing, the apparent anarchic disorder and, above all, the lack of luggage trolleys. (Had there been such things I could imagine them being inhabited by whole families as children's beds, washing lines etc.) What, he wanted to know, were the Embassy planning to do about it?

Chapter Eleven: Pets

Within a very short space of time Anna was speaking very fluent, albeit children's, Chinese and would chat for hours with Mrs. Yuan. It was through these conversations that she learnt of Anna's great love of animals, and realising that the 14th floor of a high-rise block wasn't an ideal place to keep any, she nonetheless gave her a pet of her own – a cricket in a cage. The cricket was large and the cage was a small ball made from woven strips of bamboo. Crickets traditionally brought good luck to the home, so in Chinese fashion we hung the cage in the kitchen window from whence emanated his very loud chirping. Food and water were combined in the feeding of strips of cucumber, with a warning from Mrs. Yuan to mind your fingers when putting it through the holes in the cage, as a cricket could give you a nasty bite. The sound of his biting into the cucumber was warning enough of the sharpness of his teeth! At one time crickets would be kept not in these cages, but in hollowed out gourds or wooden imitation gourds with ornately carved stoppers to provide ventilation and prevent escape. Mrs. Yuan's father was a great lover of these insects, and would keep 20 or 30 of them in containers hanging inside his jacket to keep them warm. Sooner him than me – the cricket frankly gave me the creeps, but we still felt rather sorry for him, being confined to such a small area. Thinking to give him a better quality of life, we carefully cut a hole in the bamboo cage and released him into a birdcage. To our horror what we'd thought of as a large grasshopper bore more resemblance to something out of 'Quatermass and the Pit'; once not squashed into a small space he revealed himself as enormous. He could squeeze through small spaces, despite his size, and started to climb through the bars. I grabbed a wooden ruler with which to push him back in, but he held onto it firmly and I could actually feel him pulling the ruler into the cage. Mike rushed for a glass fish tank we had stored in a cupboard and managed to transfer him into that, covering the tank with a heavy insect screen hastily removed from one of the windows. All went well for a couple of days until Anna worried that he wasn't getting enough air and moved the insect screen – "only a tiny crack"! That was enough – he escaped. Bearing even more resemblance to a horror film, we scoured the flat in search of the 'creature from hell'. Imagine getting into bed and feeling something moving by your toes. Why couldn't Anna have liked dolls instead of animals? He was eventually discovered down the back of a kitchen cupboard and Mike, demanding a medal for bravery, managed to trap him and drove him off to Ritan Park where Mike released him when no one was watching (quite a feat in the inquisitive Chinese environment).

We never told Mrs. Yuan the full story of the cricket, just that we released it because Anna was worried about it being kept in such a small cage; a sentiment the Chinese genuinely couldn't comprehend. Our euphoria at being rid of the beast was shortlived: within a day a replacement was produced – a beetle, about 5 inches long and with a hard, black, shiny back. "This one you'll all be quite happy with" Mrs. Yuan explained. "It doesn't have to be kept confined in any sort of a cage, you just place it on the fly screen at the window and there it will hang quite happily for ever, with just occasional feeding." It was all very well for her to assure me that it would stay where put, but I couldn't take my eyes off it in case it did decide to go walkabout. "It's also just as interesting as the cricket as it too makes a noise. Just pick it up and shake it and it'll make a loud rattling noise." If she thought I was ever going to pick it up she was very much mistaken. I lasted about three days, by which time paranoia had taken over and I was convinced that every noise I heard was the dreaded beetle heading my way. Keeping as far away as possible I managed to gently flick it off into the fish tank so recently vacated by the cricket. I would never wish harm to any creature, but I must confess that it was with some relief that we found ourselves without creepy pets when the beetle died: relief only slightly tempered by Mrs. Yuan's rather reproving speech about its not having enough air and food in the fishtank. At certain times of the year the air seemed to be a mass of large dragonflies, and the local children would catch them and tie a length of wool around each one's abdomen. As they flew about, the wool hung down, allowing their 'owners' to catch them easily but, undoubtedly thinking me incapable of looking after any insect properly, Mrs. Yuan never gave one to Anna.

Despite our lack of affection for the creepy-crawlies of this world, we were all of us great animal lovers, so I suppose it was inevitable that when one of the young secretaries returned to the U.K. we won her cat. A stray she had taken in, Mao (the Chinese word for cat) was an unneutered female with definite wildcat tendencies. The second impassioned plea came from another young lady, but one who was working in the city and was forced to give up her cat (also called Mao) when she was moved out of her rented room into an hotel. That young cat was male and as docile as they came. At the same time we had Black Mao and White Mao we also had various birds and budgies and Anna's pet white mouse with one eye (Pebbles), all of whom had to be protected from the feline hunters. The mouse had to vacate his cage and live in the fishtank, the insect screen on top being well weighted down with piles of books, and the bird cages were suspended, with various bamboo poles tied to water pipes, from the kitchen ceiling like so many chianti bottles in an Italian restaurant.

When Anna's terrapins (I'm not quite sure why we bought them on one of our trips to the bird market) developed fungal-looking patches on their skins, she wrote to the letters page of the junior RSPCA magazine for advice. For some time afterwards we boasted that they had kindly flown a private vet out to us: in fact the editor just happened to have a veterinary friend who just happened to be about to attend a pheasant symposium in Beijing, and was more than happy to come to our flat, together with his wife, and treat the terrapins. (They made a full recovery and we made two very good friends).

Further additions to the menagerie were two beautiful little fluffy chicks that Mrs. Yuan had bought off a man she spotted transporting baskets of them on the back of his bike. I ventured to ask her quite what we would do with them when they grew bigger - "you eat chicken, don't you?" was the reply, fortunately not heard by Anna. They did grow into very fine white COCKERELS, who then proceeded to crow extremely loudly at five each morning. Whereas we could turn over and go back to sleep again, our immediate – and even not too immediate neighbours –

couldn't. After several comments about the Chinese families opposite inconsiderately keeping them awake, I tried to trick the offending birds into thinking it wasn't dawn by keeping them in a dark place overnight. Unfortunately the cupboard by the rubbish chute acted rather like an amplifier and made matters ten times worse. The only solution in the end was to pick them up, one under each arm, and walk up and down rocking them gently and singing to them rather as one would to a fractious child. Sadly we eventually admitted defeat and an ayi we knew whose family lived in the country took them away – we hoped to a life of freedom and fresh air (and females!) rather than to the pot – although we'd facetiously called them 'Kentucky' and 'Tandoori' we really didn't mean it!

The International School liked to take classes on outings whenever possible, and one particular group of children had visited a commune where they had been presented with two ducklings. They were kept in a classroom at the school for a while, where they were adored by all, but ducklings do grow into rather large ducks, at which point a teacher casually remarked that she didn't quite know what would happen to them. "Oh my mum will have them" – and no guess as to whose child said that! The Embassy carpenter made us some very nice cages, they ('Bombay' and 'A l'Orange') lived on the balcony with the chickens and had a swim in the bath every day. (Yes, Anna often joined them.)

You'd really think that we'd have drawn the line there, but we did have several large balconies and the Embassy carpenter was happy to make us any number of large cages, at a reasonable price, so it seemed less silly than it sounds in retrospect to buy Anna a couple of rabbits. It took a while to explain to the peasant lady with a box of young rabbits tied to the rear of her bike, that we definitely didn't want to breed them for food, and wanted two females. They lived in Anna's bedroom at first and later on they joined the chickens and ducks on the balcony, and were lovely.

In was in early December that Mike received the most desperate of pleas from the Italian Naval Attaché. His Ambassador's wife (a woman after our own hearts) had rescued a tiny white rabbit from a carpet factory (no idea what it was doing there, unless being fattened up for Spring Festival), and as their tour of duty in Beijing was approaching its end she had detailed off the Navy to find the rabbit a new home. He was desperate and had heard that we kept various animals ourselves. After a good deal of resistance, we finally took pity on the distraught man and I agreed to visit the Ambassador's wife – I was to be interviewed to see if I would make a suitable 'foster mother'. The Italian Residence was straight out of 'Homes and Gardens' and I felt decidedly underdressed, even to visit a rabbit, and unsure as to whether I should step on the exotic carpets or skirt round them. She was a lovely person and the rabbit was spoilt rotten, having her own little courtyard with grass and bamboo growing, and access to a small dining room where she ate titbits from the table if the Ambassador and his wife were dining alone. The rabbit, Rosina, even had Luigi, one of the staff, designated to her welfare. They seemed happy enough that I would look after her, but just wanted to first see where she'd be living, which they would do the very next morning.

In the summer months I used to hose down the balcony every day (it having drain holes), but it was the middle of winter. The ducks had splashed the water from the drinking bowls, the many animals had crapped and peed and the whole had frozen over: it didn't smell of course, being solid ice, but it sure didn't look too good for the Ambassador's wife and Luigi to inspect. Muffled in coats, hats and gloves against the extreme cold we spent an unusual evening armed with hammers and chisels chipping away at an inch thick layer of rock-hard, frozen muck. We passed inspection and Rosina came to join us, the patches of fur she lost in the first few scuffles with the other rabbits eventually growing back again.

The ready availability of a vet was something we had always rather taken for granted and we didn't realise quite how much until we came to the problem of two young cats of different sexes. After a great deal of investigation we discovered a vet some way out in the suburbs who was reported to be willing to deal with foreigners, and spoke some English. With help from an interpreter I made an appointment for Black Mao (the female) to be speyed, as I had been assured that it would calm her down and she'd become more of a domesticated than a wild cat. The surgery appeared all a bit 'barefoot' – old metal tables and rows of implements – but the vet lady seemed to know what she was talking about and told me to return later in the day to collect the cat after the operation. It had all seemed too easy, and our slight doubts that all would go smoothly were confirmed when I returned to be told that they'd been unable to operate. Mao had an allergy to anaesthetic and instead of putting her out she went as high as a kite and it had taken two vets two hours to catch her! Whether that was indeed the case, or whether they just couldn't handle an extremely angry, fierce and frightened feline I don't know, but we admitted defeat and booked White Mao in for castration instead. I naively expected to deliver him in the morning and collect him later in the day, but for such a 'simple' operation they didn't deem it necessary for him to stay at the vet's, and it was a case of all hands to the wheel. Mao was sedated and secured to a table, each of his legs tied to the table legs. Another 'customer' was called in from the waiting room and he and I were instructed to hold him still while the vet operated and we watched. With incredible speed it was all over and, with no thought of time to recuperate, Mao and I were shown out.

As the time of our departure from China loomed closer, we were naturally concerned as to what would happen to the animals, but help was at hand from our good friends at the Milu Deer Reserve. We arrived there one Sunday with three rabbits, one duck (one had sadly died by that time), and Black Mao. The rabbits were put in a small deer pen, from which they promptly escaped and had to be transferred to an outbuilding; Mao was to live with one of the Chinese staff and earn her living catching rats, and the duck was to fulfil a mission of mercy. Two beautiful Sika deer had been sent to Milu from another part of the country, but the workmen accompanying them had no idea of an animal's needs and welfare and one of the deer had died. The remaining one was kept in a small enclosure to allow her to slowly settle down in her new surroundings, but she was very frightened and lonely. The duck was put in the adjoining enclosure and for the first time since her arrival the Sika took an interest in something, and was obviously glad of the company.

White Mao was taken on by our successors and Mrs. Yuan's husband, who had been very ill and needed a sedentary hobby, gratefully took the terrapins and some goldfish we had also accumulated. The one creature we just could not find a home for was Pebbles the mouse: he was either seen as vermin or something to be afraid of. As a last resort we took him out to a derelict Ming Tomb and released him deep into a crack in the side of an Emperor's last resting place.

Apart from the Italians, we weren't quite alone in our keeping of animals, although we were the only people we knew who managed it living on the 14th floor of a block of flats. In the garden of the first compound we lived in, we one night heard the sound of bleating, and when we looked out saw a lamb and a kid (goat) tethered to a tree. There they stayed for several days, and were constantly being stroked and cuddled by all the children, but they were unfortunately not pets, but being kept ready for slaughter at a religious festival. Their eventual demise was unseen by us, the slaughtering being carried out most unobtrusively - there had been many complaints one year when the goat had escaped mid-ceremony and dashed around the compound leaving a trail of blood. It had eventually run in to someone's flat and died messily on her carpet.

One of the British Ambassadors in Beijing during our time there had two young sons who were one day, on their travels, given a duckling by a farmer. He thought they would eat it once it was big enough but, naturally, it became a much-loved pet. It was given free run of the large Residence garden, but was always shut in at night, but one evening was left out slightly later than usual and was found with a terrible neck injury, having been attacked by some wild animal. At that time there were no known vets, so they rang the Embassy nurse to ask her the kindest way to put the poor duck to sleep. She advised a massive dose of paracetamol, but the Residence medicine cabinet only had aspirin, so a large dose of that was administered instead. To everyone's amazement it failed to have the expected effect: far from dying, the duck rallied and within a few days he was up and about (the aspirin having dissolved the blood clot that was preventing his recovery). He always walked with a limp, and couldn't hold his head straight, but was as happy a duck as you'd see anywhere – and was taken back to the U.K. with them when they left. There will hopefully always be a memorial to Ping the duck in the Residence dining room. When new wallpaper was needed it was specially ordered and hand painted with beautiful Chinese scenes, and in one panel, amongst lotus flowers and mandarin ducks there was painted a beautiful mallard – Ping himself.

Chapter Twelve: Tian an Men   June 1989

Tian An Men in June 1989 has now been written into the history books as a major event in the history of modern China. We had a 'grandstand' view of much of what happened, as recorded in my diary of the events:

15 April

   Hu Yaobang dies today, causing a feeling of loss amongst the student population here as he was seen as sympathetic to their desire for greater democracy.

22 April

   What we thought might be a brief period of mourning still continues, only now the students are more vociferous in their demands for reforms, especially the stamping out of corruption. It seems that there had been an undercurrent of discontent for some time and Hu's death has simply been the catalyst to bring it out in to the open. There are groups of young people daring to demonstrate their feelings in public. I would have thought they would have been stopped by the police, but the government has always had a more lenient attitude to students, as throughout China's history many great new movements have originated from the universities.

28 April

   Driving home from an artist friend's flat situated to the west of the city, we meet a solid wall of students on bicycles heading for Tian An Men Square and have to wait five minutes or more for them to pass by. It is a cross between a carnival and a giant street party: they wave and sing goodnaturedly and it is more a noisy way of making their point than the sort of thing you associate with a demonstration. The traffic police whom you would normally expect to be in evidence trying to keep the traffic moving seem to have disappeared, but as we follow on behind we see that the cyclists have organised themselves very efficiently and have students positioned at major crossings, who do as good a job as the police.

30 April

The demonstrations have escalated and we see hundreds of students on bikes and on foot marching around the streets and heading for the square, but at all times they are incredibly orderly, keeping carefully to the sides of the roads so as to disrupt the traffic as little as possible. For the first time today I see a police presence: as marchers are heading off the ring road and onto the flyover leading onto Chang An, about 50 police form up in two lines across the slip road to stop them. The marchers stop and their leaders start to argue with the policemen in charge, but within minutes the students simply step over the low railings onto the ornamental gardens and bypass the police and continue on their way. The effort to stop them is token – the police obviously have orders to be seen doing something, but nothing to antagonise the demonstrators. One policeman is hurt in the confrontation, but not at the hands of a student: he trips over the railings and cuts his leg on the metal.

13 May

The situation is getting suddenly more serious: the students aren't going to back down in their fight for greater democracy and have called a hunger strike amongst all the hundreds of them now camping in makeshift tents in the square.

15 May

The demonstrators' timing is perfect – Gorbachev arrives today and the government are being well and truly humiliated. Not only can they not receive their important guest in Tian An Men Square as is normal, but the world's press are here to cover the visit, and witness the whole embarrassing affair. The troubles are very centralised - in the outskirts you wouldn't know there was anything going on. I take my tricycle to explore some of the hutongs to the north of Ritan Park and find a building very Middle-Eastern in looks. The gate is open and I walk into a small, quiet, flower-filled courtyard with a wall on three sides, the fourth side being a small mosque. It is obviously still used today, as a watchman invites me to remove my shoes and enter. I hadn't realised that there was still an active Muslim community here.

17 May

On the way back from the children's lessons at the gymnasium today we are held up as usual by streams of student demonstrators on bicycles. Every major road and cycle track seems to be thick with them, but they are still all very orderly and never obstruct the traffic unnecessarily. They seem to spend all day taking turns circumnavigating the city carrying banners and chanting, and then return to the square to spend the night. Many of those on hunger strike are causing concern and are being monitored by teams of doctors, and throughout the day and night we are increasingly hearing the wail of ambulance sirens as one of them becomes dangerously weak and is removed to hospital. For some reason I can't put my finger on the feeling on the streets this evening as I wait to drive home seems to have lost its carnival atmosphere and has been replaced by an almost ominous air. Whereas I have always felt quite happy driving through the throngs of cyclists, I have a funny feeling that today they might suddenly turn nasty. Yet once home, gazing out at a wonderful sunset and the golden reflection on the only skyscraper to the east of us, I feel I must have imagined it.

18 May

We have just heard from the Embassy that we are advised not to go into areas where there are demonstrators as, although they still appear friendly, there is a feeling that the mood could change. The possible reason for this is that the students now appear to have been joined by workers who may be of a more militant frame of mind.

Anna and a friend have been doing a science project at school involving hatching chicken eggs, and tonight the eggs appear to be about to hatch. Great timing! The school is on the road to the airport, miles from the city centre, so I decide to risk a run out there this evening to video the great event. I go armed with sleeping bags, in case it involves a long wait, and I have also rehearsed the Chinese for "I am going to the school because the eggs are hatching" in case I am stopped. When we arrive, one of the eggs has a small crack, but that appears to be all that is going to happen – perhaps the chicks have gone back to sleep again. We wait for a few hours, but as still nothing is moving, decide to go home and return tomorrow. By this time it is dark, and as we near the city the major crossroads is blocked with buses parked across the road. A student waves us down and shines his torch round the inside of the car to make sure we aren't transporting any police or army personnel. With a happy smile and a farewell wave he directs us into the cycle track, around the barricade, and on our way. It is true that the students are doing a good job as traffic policemen; whether because there aren't as many cars on the road I don't know, but the traffic certainly seems to be flowing unusually smoothly these days.

19 May

As more and more people are marching, and the square gets more crowded and dirtier (apart from anything else there aren't nearly enough toilets in the area for this number of people) it seems inevitable that the government must act. There is a stalemate as regards talks between the two sides, and whereas the students are more leniently tolerated, any sort of uprising amongst the workers is viewed more seriously. It is of no surprise to us to hear the rumour that troops may well be sent in. And still the eerie wail of ambulances to and from the square.

20 May

In an attempt to get things on the road to normality Martial Law is declared, but surprisingly, no curfew is imposed.

22 May

The Martial Law enforcement troops that have been sent into the city seem to be failing in their objective, as an ever-increasing number of ordinary people seem to be joining the demonstrators, and buses are seized and roadblocks set up everywhere. The cry of the people seems to be that these are the PEOPLE'S Liberation Army and therefore should be for the people not against them. As the troops arrive at the roadblocks they are reasoned with, then harangued and then amazingly either stay put or withdraw. Yet more humiliation for the leaders it seems. The lorries aren't allowed to move, but once they've decided not to put up a fight, the soldiers are treated extremely well by their 'captors', who supply them with food, fruit and drinks.

25 May

The feeling on the streets is rather nasty now and some sort of major confrontation is inevitable. There is one potentially disastrous event today, when the massed demonstrators stop a large convoy of Air Force transporters carrying what they believe to be tear gas canisters (for use against them). After some time the drivers eventually persuade the crowd to let them continue on their way. To the Attachés' more practised eyes the 'canisters' appear to be large surface-to-air missiles, complete with fuel and warheads. The outcome, had the crowd decided to set fire to them, doesn't bear thinking about. It is an illustration of the lack of communication between the various departments and army etc. that such a convoy should ever have been allowed to cross the city in such potentially volatile times.

26 May

What with those taken to hospital during the hunger strike, and extremely heavy rain, Tian An Men Square is emptying somewhat and the demonstrators seem less intense and enthusiastic than of late. This would seem the opportune moment for the government to go in and put an end to the whole affair, which we think they are doing when, during the night, we hear a low throbbing noise in the distance. We stay up on the balcony all night to see what will happen – it's either a very silent operation or nothing takes place; we shall have to wait and see.

2 June

There is a temple to the south of the square which I have been meaning to visit for some time, and as things are quiet I drive off there today. It is down a winding back street, and is nothing special in the way of a temple, but it does have the most beautiful little courtyard gardens and a lovely display of roses. I carefully avoid going near the centre of town but on the way home I am directed around the square by the one-way system. The tents are looking very tatty now and the whole place looks a mess. I daren't stop the car, but driving slowly I get a glimpse of the Goddess of Democracy statue the students have made, and the students milling around. It is a good indication of how very localised the trouble is: just a short distance away, in the temple, all is as normal.

3 June

We are woken very early in the morning by a phone call from another Embassy member telling us to look out of our window. Jogging silently along Chang An in the direction of Tian An Men we see columns of troops. They have no caps on, or jackets, but carry backpacks, and on their feet are rubber-soled shoes, presumably so they can get to the square without being detected. There appear to be several thousand of them. Their attempts at creeping in unnoticed fail: the lookouts posted at all intersections get enough notice to pedal ahead frantically on their bikes to warn those in the square. I don't see what good that can do; this many troops must surely get through. By daylight it becomes clear that so many people turned out in opposition that the troops were turned away. Mike cycles around to see what's happening and finds groups of bewildered and humiliated soldiers wandering around in the vicinity of the Observatory. There are very few Officers in evidence and two NCOs are trying to rustle up enough loose change to make a phone call (to their base to ask for instructions?) Eventually an order must come through as they suddenly head back in the direction they'd come from.

It's now 5 pm and we've noticed more and more people heading in the direction of the square. Just outside our flats a convoy of about 50 army trucks are stopped by the people, together with many on the flyover on Chang An. There are so many people that I have grave doubts as to the strength of the flyover itself and envisage the horror of its collapsing. Five open civilian trucks now approach, their backs filled with workers wearing yellow hardhats. Some of the crowd are curious, or maybe suspicious, and stop the first truck, to look in the back. When they see not builders' tools, but batons, riot shields and crates of soft drinks their anger flares and the contents are thrown out. The 'workmen' (almost certainly militia in disguise) don't wait around to suffer the same fate: amongst the debris of broken drink bottles, they jump from the trucks and run for it.

4 June

It has started. At 12.30am an Armed Personnel Carrier passes our compound heading west, towards the square, pursued by locals on bikes and on foot. A group of girls aged about 18 hold hands in a line across the road as the vehicle, grinding up the road surface, approaches. Just as it seems it must crush them they break ranks and run, much to everyone's relief. We learn that a crowd are enraged because the APC had earlier crushed a cyclist: maybe it had been a deliberate act, or maybe the driver had been 'shut down for action' and therefore had very limited vision and genuinely didn't see him. Some 'captured' army trucks have been pulled across the road as a barricade, but they are no match for the APC which rams them and pushes them aside, continuing towards the square. It is quite likely that there are soldiers still in the trucks, being too frightened of the crowd to risk leaving: in which case there must have been some serious injuries sustained.

Throughout the night, spent on the balcony, we see the glow of fires to the west (it must be that the mob are setting fire to captured vehicles) and hear explosions as petrol tanks ignite. The sky is periodically illuminated with tracer fire from the direction of the square – this is the battle we had expected, but had hoped would be averted.

In the early hours of the morning we hear the noise of heavy engines approaching from the east and suddenly the crowds on the flyover begin to run and scatter in any direction in which they can find an escape route. Into our view rumbles the first tank: it pauses briefly to line itself up and then rams a barricade of buses. It backs up and with an even more sickening sound of tearing metal it's through and on its way to Tian An Men. More tanks and APCs follow, some tanks sideswiping the wrecked buses and missing the gap – it seems that it is very hard to steer a tank accurately when you're shut down for action. No attempt has been made to hide the action from the foreigners: the arc lights on the flyover are still switched on and we are able to video it all. Occasionally one of the many tanks takes a wrong turning and heads off down another road. One such ends up in the garden directly below us and the crowd moves in for the kill – literally. With much grinding of gears and destruction of trees, flowerbeds and fencing the tank gets away. As other APCs try to rejoin Chang An, the leader stops to avoid hitting a taxi (coming the wrong way). To the applause of the onlookers below, the second APC rams straight into the back of the leading one!

7am. It has been a long night and all now seems quiet, so I lie down on the bed for a sleep. Within a minute the phone rings. Jonathan has been at the Cub Scout campout, fortunately held in the grounds of the American Embassy. As the tanks rolled in to the city the boys were quickly removed from their tents on the lawn (one boy under each arm of a US Marine) and taken into a secure room inside the building. There they were guarded by a Marine in full battle dress – it was the best campout ever! Now there is the problem of getting all the boys safely to their own homes – it seems there is no fighting on the streets now, so I drive off to collect him and some of his friends and get them all to their respective homes.

During the day we have a worried visit from our neighbour: the student broadcasts have been heard to report that the British Naval Attaché has been injured near the square. He is relieved to find Mike at home, and fit. We decide that it is probably the misquoting of a name and the injured party is most likely to be the journalist Michael Fathers, not the Attaché Michael Farr.

5 June

News is gradually filtering through of the clearing of the square and heavy fighting to the west of the city. Many of the tanks and their crews come from a long way outside Beijing and therefore know nothing of the earlier student demonstrations nor of the reasons behind this 'uprising'. (It is very easy in this country to ensure that people only hear what you want them to). They have merely been told that there is 'turmoil' in the capital and anarchy rules on the streets. It is really quite understandable then that when they enter the city and are attacked viciously by the populace that they retaliate to restore order and protect themselves. In this latter, they are not always successful and quite a few soldiers die at the hands of the masses, or are incinerated within their vehicles. It appears that some of the worst fighting and greatest casualties on both sides have occurred in the streets to the west, leading into Tian An Men rather than in the square itself, and the majority of the students reportedly left the square before the army takes over.

The Embassy is having a frantic day with switchboards jammed with calls from relatives and the media. Amongst the most insistent callers are a small group of journalists from Hong Kong who insist that someone be sent to help them. They are in the Peking Hotel, which is surrounded by soldiers and tanks – not because the hotel is under siege, but because it is so near to the square. The Embassy advice is to stay put or, if they really feel they are seriously threatened, to follow the path of some other journalists and climb over the back wall where there are no soldiers, and make their way along the hutongs to a safer position further from the action. The journalists seem to think that we are refusing to help them because they're from Hong Kong rather than the U.K., but there really is no one at the Embassy able to go at this time and 'rescue' them – there are others, such as British students at the universities, who are in much greater potential danger from the army/student fighting, and we need to move them first. It's funny to think that most journalists are fighting to get INTO the city.

Looking out from the front balcony of our flat we see a city in turmoil, yet from the back windows just a few yards' distant, there is a scene of peace and utter normality, as people cycle to work and walk in the park. Even where there are tanks, people seem to be oblivious to any danger - they are even taking their children out for a walk to see them. As for those who live a distance away, it is all as if it is happening in another world: I have phone calls from the Lido Hotel from friends asking me what on earth is going on. There are rumours that the British Embassy has been set on fire, but I assure them that I can see it from the window, and it is still there, unscathed. We are getting less information ourselves now: the various Defence Attachés who were out and about kept in touch with each other by means of walkie-talkies, but have stopped using them now in case the army overhears and thinks they are passing information to the demonstrators.

The British Council does a wonderful job in collecting up all the British students from universities both near and far, and housing them with Embassy families. We have four girls with us – all very upset and unwilling to leave, but realising the necessity of it. If we don't get them out now and the situation deteriorates even more we may not be able to help. We have been warned now not to go out onto the balconies or we will be shot at – a warning we take seriously, especially when Mrs. Yuan tells us of an old lady in San Li Tunr who ignored the warning and was killed. So we now pull all the curtains and live a cave-like existence keeping well away from the windows just in case we cast shadows. From some reason I once bought a catering size tin of baked beans from the Embassy shop and these, together with next Christmas's turkey, provide enough food for us all for the day. We never seem to get a meal without some interruption – sometimes a phone call but more usually loud shooting outside. I have remained pretty well impartial throughout, not being able to express an opinion without all the facts, but I finally lose my temper with the whole thing when we can't even eat supper in peace. As we sit down to roast turkey, the firing starts and we have to remove to the hallway, away from any outside walls. As I grab my plate I utter the immortal words "Up yours, Li Peng!" (Li Peng being one of the chief government leaders in this affair).

As we lie down in sleeping bags and blankets on the hall floor we start to tell jokes (Jonathan and Anna's favourite pastime) and Jonathan entertains us with his very realistic impersonations of machines, cars etc. When he does his 'machine gun' we realise just how tense we feel underneath – although it's just a small noise and a long way from the outside world we still tell him not to do that one in case someone hears us!

Ayatollah Khomeni dies today – but what should be an important piece of world news is rather overshadowed by the events in Beijing.

6 June

The British students are flown back to the U.K. today, and Mrs. Yuan and Mr. Zhang turn up for work. Mr. Zhang has had a lucky escape:

every evening after work he had been going to the square to join the 'party', as it was at that time. Fortunately on the nights of 3rd and 4th he was away at Beidaihe with some friends, otherwise he would have been in the middle of it all. Even those onlookers who ran from the tanks can often be traced if they left their bikes parked nearby: as every bike is licensed the owners can easily be found, and your very presence in the area labels you as a supporter of the mob. Convoys of trucks are still passing periodically – firing into the air to let everyone know they're there. One shot sounds a little close, so we send all the ayis and cooks home and tell them to stay there until it's a lot safer on the streets. Mrs. Yuan is unhappy to leave us, but is reassured by the fact that we have so many good Chinese friends who would never see us come to any harm.

Peering out gingerly through a crack in the bathroom curtain I can see about 27 tanks and APCs guarding the flyover and a lone body under a tarpaulin. Should the rumour of a civil war come to pass and these tanks start to fire we would be in a pretty vulnerable position, so we move out of the flat onto the landing area next to the lifts, thereby giving ourselves more walls to protect us from a stray tank shell. The neighbours have moved out here too, and we pool the food we can find in our respective kitchens (crawling along the floor to reach them) and have a veritable repast of a picnic. We keep the children amused with jigsaws and games – the boy upstairs keeps himself amused by letting off the fire extinguisher! We have been offered the use of another flat further into the compound and not on the front line as it were, but feel more able to cope with the rather inconvenient way of life in our own homes. Although I get a heart-stopping feeling every time I hear the lift operating, I am confident that were an armed soldier to step out of it I could speak enough Chinese to him to invite him to search the flat for revolutionaries and then to leave. As we settle down to a night on the landing floor, the only idea we have of what is really going on outside is from listening to the BBC World Service, as we daren't put our heads out there.

7 June

Some of the Diplomatic flats are fired on by soldiers – and no one can think why. It seems unlikely to be the odd stray bullet, but no one likes to delve too deeply into the possibility that certain flats are being targeted. There has never been any anti-foreign feeling throughout this whole affair, so why now? In view not just of this, but of the impossibility of getting out to buy food and the threat of interruptions of electricity and water supplies, it is decided to evacuate all non-essential personnel. Still crawling across the floor I pack a few essential clothes for myself and the children (Mike will stay here), plus the things I value most: my wedding ring, negatives of all our photos and the enamel box the Queen presented to Mike on her departure. It's funny comparing notes on what you take at a time like this: some wives are running in small circles unable to think what to do, whilst a friend of ours packs his favourite hat, a bottle or two of his favourite wine and the complete works of Shakespeare.

Before we can go to the airport the Embassy has to ensure that the BA flight coming up specially from Hong Kong has clearance to land here. This is causing all sorts of delays, and possible problems, and Mike tries to get things moving by contacting a Chinese colleague in the PLA Air Force. Whilst waiting for the go-ahead to evacuate I try to leave everything in the flat in as good order as I can, allowing for the fact that Mike may get marooned in the Embassy and not get back here for a while. The cats should survive quite a few days on the turkey carcass and washing up bowl of water I put in the middle of the kitchen floor, as should the terrapins with an extra handful of food. The chicks (they hatched finally and now we have to look after them as the school's shut), will have to fend for themselves on what seed I have. After a brief deliberation Anna and I open up all the bird cages and let the occupants fly free out of the kitchen window (away from the tanks). Mike rings to see if we're ready, and says they have just had an amusing incident at the Embassy. Seeing that things might get difficult, he had some days ago written up an emergency evacuation plan. Several other

Embassies also took this precaution, and the Assistant Canadian Defence Attaché asked Mike for advice. Mike suggested giving him a copy or ours to rewrite and alter as suited their use, which the Attaché did, but he forgot to alter the words 'proceed to the British Embassy' to read 'proceed to the Canadian Embassy'. There was momentary consternation when a whole lot of Canadians with suitcases turned up at our Embassy door! Still waiting for the call to go I am surprised to hear instead from a very distressed Sri Lankan lady. It seems she has gone through the diplomatic phone list calling anyone who might answer or be able to help, and had got me. She and several other Sri Lankans are hiding in the garden of the other, older diplomatic compound, terrified of going out onto the streets where the tanks are. For some political reason I can't make out, she says her Embassy won't give them shelter or help, and she's worried that all the foreigners will evacuate and they'll be left behind. She begs me to ask the British Ambassador to contact the government in Sri Lanka and bring their plight to public notice. All I can do is try to reassure her that if she stays inside a diplomatic compound she's safer than she would be anywhere else and promise her that I'll pass her message on to our Embassy. The next phone call I expect to be from Mike, but it is his Air Force contact: he has been unable to get through to the Embassy but asks me to pass the message on – flight clearance has been arranged. I thank him for his help, most genuinely, and his reply nearly reduces me to tears – "We are friends, and always will be." Those words say it all: how desperately I don't want to leave here, not knowing if I can ever return.

During our wait, the Army have apparently been hunting a sniper (explaining the shots fired at our buildings?) and at one time thought he was firing at them from the newly built World Trade Centre. Just in case, they fired shots, breaking a large number of extremely expensive reflective glass windows. When it is explained to them by a doorkeeper there that as none of the windows open there could be no sniper, they turn their attention to our area. When I look, cautiously, out of the kitchen window I see a line of armed soldiers running along the perimeter fence towards our flats, and the compound gates locked and guarded. We are trapped inside. Mike rings for an update of the situation, and we sit and wait for the next move. After what seems an eternity he rings again: all the Ambassadors with nationals inside have protested strongly to the highest authorities they have access to, and the troops are withdrawn. Before anyone can change their minds, we load our small travelling bags into the Range Rover and head for the Embassy. There we form up into a convoy with lead cars draped in Union Jacks, just so everyone knows we're diplomats. Some of the party are glad to be leaving, some hate to go, but after the cars are all loaded and the children all given chocolate by the unflappable Lady Donald, we begin our drive to the airport. There is a carefully worked out system of signalling in case of trouble – the convoy must keep together and not be split up. About half way the car lights behind flash, we have to stop. Leaving the engine running and carefully checking all round, Mike goes to investigate: one of the small children just couldn't wait and had to stop for a pee! It's uncanny how normal life is this side of the city: no tanks, no sign of any kind of trouble, and residents and farmers just carrying on their normal, everyday lives as if nothing has happened. But then I suppose to them nothing has happened.

At the airport we meet up with other British nationals who have been brought in from all over the area. One lady and her children live at one of the universities, where she teaches English, but were away at Beidaihe for two weeks. When they arrived back at the railway station they couldn't think what had happened – no news had reached them and they were met by scenes of carnage: wrecked and burnt out buses and trucks, soldiers wielding guns. They finally found a taxi but the driver laughed nervously when asked to take them to the university. When he explained to them a little of what had happened they agreed with his suggestion of going to the Embassy instead. Their passports are still in their rooms, but no one is going to stop them leaving the country right now! As we wait around for the plane, a box of crisps from the Embassy shop is broken open for the children and the Head of Chancery organises, and plays, games with them. There are alterations going on at the airport and quite unexpectedly a large sheet of corrugated metal falls with a loud clatter – it is indicative of the nervous tension we have all been under that we jump like startled rabbits at the sound.

Sitting on the plane with a delicious meal in front of me it seems so unreal, and when the TV news is shown on the video screen we get a clear view for the first time of the tanks that were just outside our curtained window.

10 June

We are staying with kind and welcoming friends in HMS Tamar, the Royal Navy base in Hong Kong. Mike rings to say that by the time they had returned from seeing us all off, all the tanks had withdrawn: had it happened sooner I would never have agreed to leave, although the situation is still highly unstable. Those left behind have got into a routine of living and dining (thanks to Lady Donald and the Residence cooks) at the Embassy, but they are now able to return to their flats at night. This is proving to be advisable as there have been a few cases of burglary in the mostly empty blocks. One of the flats below us was broken into but the intruders got more than they bargained for when the very large African resident awoke (stark naked) and chased them. Mike has had his own chases too: one of the terrapins somehow managed to escape from the tank and it took him hours to eventually find it hiding under a radiator.

Watching the many news programmes, reports and documentaries about the happenings in Beijing, I wonder if the truth will ever be clear. Was there really a 'massacre' in the square, or had, as we heard, most of the students at least left before the tanks rolled in? There were certainly many casualties, but were a large number of soldiers also brutally attacked and killed, and did they believe they were subduing a real revolution? There were certainly some breakdowns in communication and, it seems, some pretty opposed views within the leadership itself. One thing that horrifies me is the overseas news film shown on television: interviewers ask students and the man in the street what they think about the government's actions in sending in the troops. Those interviewed innocently give their views unaware that film of their faces, once shown on television, and if they say anything anti-government, will soon be used to identify them as 'black hands'. Their freedom will be short lived – and all for the sake of a good story.

23 June

We're glad to be back and all is quiet, although we are still advised not to go out at night as cars are still being stopped and searched and shots can still be heard from time to time.

18 July

On the surface life here goes on much the same, but people are frightened to talk of the past. Mr. Zhang would like to ask us about it, but Mrs. Yuan stops him; she must remember the repercussions and recriminations of idle chatter during the Cultural Revolution. Friends living in the country seemed to have been kept almost totally in the dark about the whole affair, and they too dare not even mention it. It is unnatural to have lived through a time like that together, yet be unable to talk about it. All official social contact with the Chinese has been stopped and there are stories of continuing arrests as more people are being traced back to their presence in the square or at the sites of confrontation on that fateful night. I hear that there are boxes appearing in offices and factories into which you can, anonymously, name people you know to have been involved in the turmoil: what a temptation to cause trouble for an innocent personal enemy! The relentless arrests and trials are in some ways more frightening than the actual violence of June itself, and some evenings shots can be heard quite clearly as, presumably, the guilty are executed. I hear of a young man who was arrested but eventually, with a lot of help from his work unit, proved innocent of any involvement at all. 'Bound over' to keep out of trouble for six months he is too terrified to even step foot out of his own front door in case he draws attention to himself.

24 July

Today is the first reception we have been to since June where Chinese guests known to us attend, and it is awful. They have been instructed not to have contact with military Attachés and can only answer our "how are you?" with a brief "fine", before moving off. It is so sad: these are people who just a couple of months ago were like friends. We are due to go on our mid-tour leave soon, and it is perhaps best that we are leaving for a while. We can only hope that by the time we return we may be able to rescue at least some of the good relations and friendships we once had.

9 September

Although many of our Chinese friends have to be wary of too much contact with us, there is a slightly more relaxed feeling here now than in July, and visitors are obviously expected to come back, as work on tourist sites and hotels continues. Whilst unwilling to discuss them in any detail, it is interesting to see different reactions to the events of June. An older friend feels that she ought to have some opinion about it all but, selfishly she admits, as long as none of her family is in any way involved she is happy to let it all be forgotten as quickly as possible. A young friend obviously feels sympathy for the pro-democracy, anti-corruption movement as he sees it, and regrets its 'failure'. When asked if he doesn't think that changes will come naturally when the older leaders are eventually replaced with those of his generation, his depressed reply is that once anyone gets power they become as corrupt as the rest. Hopefully his lack of hope is temporary.

It would be all too easy to forget Tian An Men, 1989, but for one couple I suspect it is etched in their memories forever: during the night of 3rd June a Norwegian resident went into labour and was rushed to the Capital Hospital. There, amidst the many casualties of the fighting she gave birth to a son. Some said he should be christened 'Martial Law'.

Chapter Thirteen: Adoption

In November 1989 a Canadian couple we knew were seriously considering adopting a child (they had none) and had heard that in a home for handicapped children in Beijing there were one or two 'normal', healthy children. They asked Mike and I, having two birth children and one adopted, and speaking some Chinese, to accompany them. We went there, together with the Embassy nurse and an interpreter friend of the Canadians. We were met by the Director, who first told us about the home and then offered us the customary mugs of tea, making sure we were seated where we could not fail to see the box marked 'donations'. He then took us on a tour. The buildings were stark, cold and concrete and rather depressing, but in direct contrast were the nurses/caregivers who more than made up for the shortfalls in the fabric of the place with the deep love they felt for, and showed to, their charges. On the first floor that we visited we were met by a deluge of toddlers, round as dumplings in their padded, split-crotched trousers and jackets (it was very cold in there) all calling "mummy" and raising their arms up, begging to be carried. Finally dragging ourselves away, we went to the 'baby' rooms. Rows of metal cots lined the walls of the rooms, each with its own little wrapped up bundle. Seeing babies swaddled so tightly they were unable to move, often distressed foreign visitors used to a culture that allowed babies freedom of movement, but to Chinese mothers it seemed frightening to a baby to be surrounded by such wide open spaces and much more secure to be either held tightly by a mother or at least swaddled. Whatever the best way, these babies seemed quite content. Some of the more able, slightly older children were sitting or standing but it was sad to see that there're just weren't enough of those wonderful helpers to go around, so no child could ever get the attention it deserved. Even at meal times one large bowl of rice or noodles with minced meat and vegetables was served up per room of eight or ten children. The ayi started with the first child and fed it from a spoon, then on to the next child until they all had some, then back to the beginning again. We asked why they all had shaved heads, giving them the look of baby PLA soldiers or Dickensian convicts. Apparently it was to halt the invasion of head lice, and to make washing all those children easier.

Most of the children there were severely mentally handicapped, some had less drastic physical handicaps and there seemed to be a large proportion of spina bifida sufferers. There was a playroom for them to be taken to with special equipment, but it didn't appear to be used very much. A group of foreign residents used to visit to work with the children, introducing them to music and all sorts of activities they'd not normally have done, but when the visits stopped so too did the activities. It was very sad, but I could also see the point of view of the ayis there – it was as much as they could do to feed, wash and clean up after all the children in their care and they did take them to the playroom to move around every day. There may also have been a feeling in society as a whole that time spent teaching such children was almost wasted, as there was no future for them in the Country at that moment. Maybe as the rights of the less fortunate were brought to the fore there would be something for these children to work towards.

We were shown three healthy children, two boys and a girl – the girl having been dressed up beautifully (I suspected the home rather hoped she would be chosen, as her future prospects were considerably less rosy than for the boys). It was difficult to advise as they were all lovely, but our friends were pretty well sure it was one of the boys they wanted. While they were chatting to the Director, I wandered off into another room of babies of about a year old, and chatted to the ayi there. As I turned to look behind the open door I saw a pair of large, brown eyes staring at me with such incredible depth that they could have belonged to an adult. In fact they belonged to a little girl who raised her top half up and stared at me even more intently. I put out my hand, and she grasped my finger, still not taking her eyes off me. I was totally, utterly lost in those eyes, when Mike, the Director and one of the Canadians came in and she switched her attention to them, watching their every move almost as if she understood what was being said. "That one's not for adoption, she's not suitable". When I asked why, he explained that she had a club foot and a 'useless' leg and no one would want her as she was not perfect. Before I could think of anything to say the rest of the party returned and I had to leave – with one last look at those eyes. It was time to go, and as we all met up by the reception area, and the donations box, I casually asked Mike if he had seen the little girl behind the door in the last room. Yes, he had and yes, those eyes had bewitched him too. The Embassy nurse commented that it was such a shame to see her there, as such a physical disability as hers was curable.

When we had adopted Tom (aged 4, from Hong Kong) we were warned that children, especially from another culture and with a different language, didn't immediately respond to their new parents and that the adoptive couple could go through a very difficult time. They dreamt of a child holding out its arms lovingly and saying "mummy, daddy" when all the child did was shy away from them. Patience invariably won in the end. Then there was the problem of jealousy from the couple's own children if they had any, even ending in physical violence or tantrums and things being thrown around the room. Dear Tom had never read that book! He had settled in, like a duck to water and Anna and Jonathan adored him. We'd always in the backs of our minds thought it would be nice to adopt a girl but had, after much discussion, decided that we couldn't risk it. Tom's adoption had been so wonderful and we'd had no problems but, even if we all accepted another child, there was a very strong possibility that the new arrival wouldn't settle and would upset the others. In view of this, why then did we find ourselves discussing the little girl behind the door and wondering what future there would be for her if she couldn't be cured, but was taken away from the home? We discussed it with the other three children in great detail: what if her leg couldn't be made better, what if she never walked, but the more we talked it through, the more we realised that there was really nothing to talk about – to parody a phrase 'the eyes win': of course we would try to adopt her.

Two days after our first visit to the home found me once again sitting sipping tea with the Director and trying hard to make polite conversation: it was the longest wait in the history of mankind, for he was to tell me what he had found out about the baby. Eventually he got round to the point: her surname was Yang and her Christian name Zi Gui (Precious Child), although they weren't her true names, no one knew them, but names chosen by the home. After a bit of probing he told me that she was found abandoned and, as all attempts by the police to trace her parents had failed, yes, she was free for adoption. That proved to be the easy part – foreign adoptions were virtually unknown and there were no ground rules or precedents.

Mrs. Yuan couldn't at first understand why we wanted any more children and especially not a handicapped one, but even if not fully convinced by our explanations she nonetheless offered all possible help. (One of the ayis at the home, on the other hand, the minute she saw me return to visit Zi Gui simply said "I knew you'd be back".) Our wonderful Chinese teacher Mr. Liu really got the bit between his teeth and spent hours writing letters and making phone calls to try to advance the cause.

In early 1990 our Canadian friends returned to the home, together with Des Gurry, an Australian paediatrician who was working at the Beijing Children's Hospital, and they invited me to go along as well. Des was to take a look at the boy they had chosen to adopt, with a view to checking not only his general health, but his development. Mr. Lin, the Director, was happy enough to comply, and Des also took a look at Zi Gui's leg, although he said he was a 'pill doctor' rather than a surgeon.

Two days later an embarrassed Des rang up. When he had returned to the Children's Hospital after our visit to the home, he had asked one of his Chinese colleagues about operations on club feet, so he could give me some idea of the possibility of success. The young lady doctor, Dr. Wang, got the bit between her teeth and consulted Dr. Pan, the chief orthopaedic surgeon. Like a game of Chinese Whispers, the message had got a little distorted every time until it finally reached Des – an appointment had been made for Zi Gui to be seen at the hospital the following day. Mrs. Yuan set to on the phone to explain the problem to Mr. Lin at the home and to arrange for an ayi to accompany Zi Gui and I to the hospital, while Mike organised the Defence Section driver, Lao Li, to drive us around. With their help, all was arranged.

The Beijing Children's Hospital was a large complex of buildings to the east of Tian An Men Square, and must have been the most overcrowded and undersized hospital anywhere. It was almost physically impossible to move between the crowds waiting in Outpatients, which sadly meant that many parents put off a visit until the child's condition deteriorated, sometimes dangerously. Even those waiting for appointments were packed in, many having to stand in corridors, and the whole place was so very old-fashioned in décor and design. What was far from old-fashioned was the expertise of the medical staff, many of whom had spent some time abroad, and all of whom were as highly trained, skilful and competent as their Western counterparts. It was the lack of equipment, much of which, being imported, required payment in FEC which they didn't have, that held them back. Even so, children came from all over China for treatment there.

Doctor Pan spoke perfect English and was a charming man. He examined Zi Gui's foot and leg and said that he could operate to correct the problem, although further operations might be needed later on. I explained that I had really intended to get treatment once she was adopted, and probably in the U.K. Details such as legal guardianship etc. were of no interest to him, he was concerned that she had already started to stand on the foot and he wanted to operate sooner rather than later. His obvious determination to cure her brooked no argument, and the date for the operation was set. Somehow we had to get the go ahead from Mr. Lin.

On 15th March Dr. Wang met Zi Gui and I at the staff entrance to the hospital and showed me the back way to the wards, avoiding the crowds. The beds in the ward were metal and purely functional, and there was not a toy or a bright picture to be seen. Even the paintwork was 'institutional'. Parents were expected to take a very large part in the care of children in the hospital, feeding, washing, dressing them etc. thus freeing the overworked nurses to deal with the medical side. The operation was scheduled for the following day and I was invited to telephone for news, and to visit her every day thereafter from 2 till 4 in the afternoon. The Chinese parents were expected to put in much longer hours, those from outlying provinces staying in a hostel in the grounds, but they feared they would find it a bit difficult having a foreigner around all the time. This was a unique situation: foreign children were all treated in the foreigners' section of the Capital Hospital, but Zi Gui was still of Chinese nationality. I was therefore the first foreigner to have a child treated there.

The operation was a success and she was in plaster from toes to thigh, but seemed happy enough – until she saw me, whereupon she screamed and burst into tears. Whether she associated me with having been taken away from the only home she had ever known, or whether she was scared of a non-Chinese face, and smell, I didn't know, but for days her reaction to me was the same: she cried for the whole time that I carried her around, or even just tried to play with her. One older girl, who played with Zi Gui every day, was pleased to see me – she wanted to show me how well she could walk, a thing she had hardly been able to do before. She was so proud and hopeful of a brighter future. I asked her if she minded having been in hospital for such a long time: "Oh no, it's much better than being at home. There I'm all alone, but here I have so many other children to play with." Perhaps there wasn't such a need for toys there after all; the children certainly seemed quite happy amusing each other. After the initial reserve, the other parents were very helpful and friendly: one mother showed me where I collected Zi Gui's bowl of noodles and one father asked me to keep an eye on his child while he went outside for a smoke. The only other father in the room greeted me when I arrived, then returned to his avid reading of the Life of Lei Feng. Lei Feng was a model PLA soldier, a cross between the Good Samaritan and Robin Hood, who was to be emulated by all. His early and untimely death in an accident only added to his aura. I'd rather thought that he was no longer held up as a paragon, but perhaps some people still studied his life – or maybe it was compulsory reading for the next political meeting. If only Zi Gui would have stopped crying – it was very hard not to doubt the sense of taking on a child who didn't like you. Was it really in the best interests of the child? Fortunately when Mike visited the hospital she screamed less, and even stopped for a while when he walked up and down the corridor with her, singing the Skye Boat Song. Whether it was the deep tone or the reverberations she felt in his chest, it did the trick. Perhaps there was hope!

Doctor Pan was so pleased with progress on the leg, that he decided to send her home earlier than planned, thus presenting a problem. Where was she to go? Mr. Lin said that he thought she'd be better off with us, otherwise she'd get used to life in the home again only to have to go through the trauma of another move when the adoption took place. (He seemed to take it as read that it would go ahead). I suspected too, that the last thing the busy ayis in the home wanted was a baby in a plaster to care for, much as they loved her. Fortunately Mr. Lin worked more by common sense than bureaucracy and Zi Gui came home with us, even though she hadn't been adopted. Funnily enough, once we got her into the flat she seemed to see it as a new phase in her life, and stopped crying. She was even reasonably happy to be carried, but not to be hugged.

Maybe it was because she was living with us in a rather unique legal position, but suddenly things started to move with Zi Gui's adoption. Mr. Lin came one day to inspect our home – he had to file a report that we had suitable accommodation. He then went with Mike, Zi Gui, Mr. Liu (as interpreter) and I to a Notary's office to discuss the other conditions we had to fulfil. The office seemed to be situated in a partially converted warehouse and we reached it up steep flights of very unprepossessing, concrete stairs. We were ushered into a large, stark room with a couple of desks, bookcases and armchairs, where we were interviewed by the Notary while his assistant took notes. They had reports from the home giving more details of her past: she had been found, aged about two months, on Beijing Railway Station, at Spring Festival. If anyone wanted to leave a baby and not be noticed they would do it at that time, when up to 200,000 people a day passed through the station on their way to visit relatives. Every seat, every inch of floor, even the forecourt outside would be thick, and I mean really thick, with people. Those with a long wait between trains lay down on thick quilts to sleep, often covering themselves completely with blankets or more quilts. You could often trip over a whole family bedded down in that way, and it was a delicate and slow job to pick your way between them all. A baby left on a seat (usually in a box or makeshift container) would not be discovered until some at least of the throng had left, by which time the parents would be long gone and totally untraceable. Which is just what had happened in Zi Gui's case: she had then been handed over to the police who, because of her leg, had sent her on to the Home for Handicapped Children. It seemed a heartless thing for any mother to do, but we really couldn't judge by our standards. With the only child permitted to you being unable to live a normal life, and probably living a long way from the capital with no access to specialised medical care, and if you came from an old traditional family who still treasured boys – pressure from family could be enormous. We were grateful that she loved her baby so much that she left her somewhere she'd be found: a few years before and she'd quite likely have been killed or left to die.

The questions we were asked concerned our financial status, our home and our future plans, and we were then asked if we would be able to make certain promises if requested. Could we promise to give her equal rights with the other children, never to abuse her and never to abandon her. We assured the Notary that we would have no problem in making those assurances when the time came to apply for the adoption. It was then necessary to ascertain her date of birth: she was found on 12th February (month two) and was judged to be two months old. According to the clerk, that made her date of birth the 12th

November (month eleven). Mike was just about to point out the mathematical error when I whispered to him to say nothing – she wouldn't want a birthday too near Christmas! (In 'old' China you were considered to be one year old at birth, having spent the best part of a year alive in the womb). There was one final point to clear up before we could presumably put in our formal application to adopt. The sound of the name 'Zi Gui' could apparently be spelt in two different ways: one set of characters meaning 'Precious Child' and the other meaning 'cuckoo' – which did we want? Although the latter did appeal to our sense of humour, we naturally chose the first option. That was it then. We stood and prepared to leave. The Notary shook us warmly by the hands and declared that he had never before had the pleasure of granting such an obviously successful and happy adoption. We looked at Mr. Liu who seemed as confused as we were – it appeared we had adopted her, without realising it. Home to celebrate!

In May it was necessary to return to the Children's Hospital for Zi Gui to have her plaster removed, but the electric plaster cutter was broken ("it's Chinese" was their explanation), so an array of implements was produced. They ranged from scissors to hammer, chisel and screwdriver, and poor Zi Gui was naturally terrified by the whole thing. Eventually, as it was taking so long to get the plaster off, they decided to give her a mild dose of anaesthetic. I felt as if I had stepped back to the days of Florence Nightingale when they put a gauze mask over her nose and slowly dropped the anaesthetic onto it. It put Zi Gui under, but the smell also made me feel pretty sick. Finally it was all over and we took her home, still only half conscious. To think that a child had to be subjected to that just because there wasn't enough money to buy a plaster cutter from abroad.

To ensure that the operation performed on Zi Gui's leg continued to benefit her, she had to be fitted with a special (Denis Brown) splint, which basically consisted of a pair of shoes with a metal bar joining them yet keeping them a set distance apart, and keeping her feet at a particular angle. From what Doctor Pan said it sounded as if she would stand in a 'Charlie Chaplin' like pose! So it was off to Wangfujing to try to find a pair of ankle boots for her, but we needed two pairs as her feet weren't the same size and this proved very difficult. We could certainly get different sizes, but not in the same design – it seemed she would have to have totally different shoes on each foot. Finally finding something that we hoped would be acceptable, we went to the Orthotics factory. As we entered, we were met by a woman with a false leg tucked under her arm – presumably she was collecting it for a relative as she already had two good ones of her own. We were asked to wait our turn in the corridor whilst patients left with all sorts of artificial limbs or parts of limbs. The man who saw us explained that he would normally make such a splint in a different way from Doctor Pan's instructions (which we had written down) and asked which way did we want it done. At the risk of offending him, we chose the doctor's way – he seemed quite happy to comply, and said the splint would be ready in about ten days. It had proved hard to give our full attention to the matter in hand as at a table near us a man was being fitted with a glass eye. There on the table was a box containing eyes and he was offered one after another to try. One even rolled across the table, but was caught before it rolled onto the floor like a scene from an old horror film.

Our time for leaving China was approaching and we had all the adoption papers we needed, plus promises of a British entry visa, but we still lacked a Chinese passport and exit visa for Zi Gui, who would not be British until adopted in the U.K. We knew for a fact that getting a Chinese passport could take six months or more – time which we didn't have. What we did have were very good friends in the Public Security Bureau and, not wanting to ask special favours of them, simply asked the name of the Department we should approach with our request. Within a couple of days we were summoned, with Zi Gui, to the passport office – not that she needed to attend, but they all wanted to see her! We had had pictures of her taken at a local photographic shop, but fortunately they had not 'touched up' the final prints: portrait type photos of adults often had all the wrinkles carefully painted out! We filled out many forms – or rather, a very helpful lady filled them out and we signed them, and then with bated breath we asked her how long it would take to issue the passport. She could have said 24 months, weeks or, at best, days, but bless her she said 24 hours; undoubtedly due to our good friends at the Public Security Bureau.

Shortly before our final departure, we were visited by a lovely lady from the Ministry of Propaganda, who wished to interview us about Zi Gui. She was to write an article for the Chinese newspapers encouraging people to think about the plight of handicapped children, and pointing out how many of them had such slight problems that they could easily be given just the same chance in life as their 'normal' peers. Ours was the first foreign adoption of a handicapped child, and although we hoped she wouldn't lay too much emphasis on the 'we must emulate the foreigners' side of the case, we dearly hoped that some good might come out of her article.

Chapter Fourteen: That Was China

There was no middle of the road opinion on China – you either loved it or hated it. If you came under the latter description you could either count the days until you left or try to turn your particular part of China into a little bit of Britain. I read a wonderful story set in the days when foreign residents were able to rent disused temples and buildings in the Western Hills for weekend and holiday retreats from the intense heat of the Beijing summers. A very British wife described the original decoration of one such building – beautiful wall paintings and carvings – and then went on to explain how she'd managed to tear out the woodwork and then get wallpaper from London to cover the Chinese paintings. Together with imported pieces of furniture to replace the old Chinese ones, and English carpets and curtains, she proudly announced that were it not for the view outside you would never know that you weren't back home in her little sitting room near London. Fiction it might have been, but I suspected it was based heavily on fact in some cases. In more modern times any such wives just isolated themselves, mixing only with other foreign residents.

We were fortunate in that we loved China, good and bad, frustrating and disarming. Frustrations ranged from 'meiyou' on the milk counter to missing suitcases and rain-damaged crates, but were all far outweighed by the many Chinese friends we made, the many kindnesses and the many laughs.

"You must be tired"? Well, yes. After the round of farewell drinks, dinners and banquets we were tired and although physically packed and ready to leave, mentally and emotionally I was far from it. A country, my first impression of which had been of an unsmiling and unfriendly place, had become the country I loved and felt totally at home in. Chinese friends and I joked that I must have been Chinese in a previous existence: I felt at home, loved the food (even sea slugs), enjoyed speaking the language and, the greatest test of all, really liked watching Peking Opera! We joked – but there was one particular small, concubines' courtyard in the Forbidden City where I had a <u>really</u> uncanny feeling of having lived there before. Déjà vu? - maybe, or maybe not.

China certainly had the last word. One day in June 1990 the China Daily published the answers to the previous day's English language crossword. The first two 'across' clues had been 'man's nickname' and 'he was Klinger'. There written in place on the solution crossword were the answers - Pat Farr.

Chapter Fifteen: Six Years On

"You'll notice so many changes", "It's all changed such a lot" – those were the comments we were always getting from friends, both Chinese and British, who heard that we were returning to Beijing for a quick visit. We guessed that any changes would be around the city centre or in areas set aside for development, so it was no surprise to see the same brown earth, the same brown farms, the same brown farm roads as we flew in to Beijing airport, and the only change to the airport itself seemed to be the start of a vast new terminal building: a forest of scaffolding and a dozen or more cranes. "We apologise for the delay" came the disembodied voice of our pilot, "but as hard as we try we cannot persuade the airport authorities to let us go alongside any other arrival gate than the one designated, and that's occupied by a United Airlines plane for the next ten minutes" – no, nothing had really changed.

Not hassled by taxi drivers as in the past, we were met by a representative of the China Travel Service, at one time just about the only tour company within China but latterly just one of many. There had been an enormous increase in the number of hotels too, judging by the array of names for shuttle bus services and on display at the special reservations desk manned by a young man in very resplendent uniform positively dripping gold braid. It was heartening to see though that one of the girls at the airport information desk still drank her tea from a jamjar and her meal of rice, meat and an enormous piece of steamed bread was still consumed from a metal bowl garishly decorated with painted flowers.

The houses and shops alongside the airport road seemed unchanged, although in some areas they were fast becoming overshadowed by large buildings. According to our guide many of the new buildings were offices and hotels rather than residential centres, and housing remained in short supply. Five years back the government gave permission to those who could afford it to buy their own flats or houses rather than wait for the government or danwei (work unit) to allocate one. I imagine few were able to raise anywhere near enough to take up the rather expensive option.

One big change was on the roads, which were *far* busier: the number of cars had risen dramatically to 2 million, and bicycles to 8 million and traffic jams had become the norm rather than the exception. (We were surprised that the standard of driving was much better than we would have expected.) The reason for this was the lifting of the restrictions on private car ownership. If a medium priced car cost around £10,000 then there was obviously a lot more money around, as so many private individuals could afford to buy one. Such as could, were probably managerial level or in business and I just hoped that other professionals such as doctors, teachers etc. were also reaping the benefits of the new prosperity. It did also, unfortunately, seem to highlight the differences between worker and manager: previously one might have had a slightly better home, more choice of food etc., but at least they *both* rode a bicycle to work. Presumably the increase in vehicles had also given rise to a whole new employment infrastructure: driving instructors and examiners, car park attendants, maybe one day traffic wardens? One lovely touch was that the toll booths across the airport road, far from being purely functional, were built as brightly painted, traditional Chinese archways.

Another restriction that had been lifted was that you could choose your career rather than have one allocated, but with that new freedom had come the disadvantage that it was not always easy to find work once you had left school or college. At least before, you had been guaranteed a job, although not necessarily one that you'd choose. We met, quite by chance, 'pigtails of milk' who told us that she'd been married for about seven years and that her husband had gone to Canada to work. She hadn't seen him for six years and as long as she was alone she couldn't apply for a flat and had to live with her parents. Life was still difficult for some.

'Regional' might have been a better word than 'superficial' to describe the changes, although the 'regions' were small. Going back to the Jian Guo Men Wai area, where we had lived and whose flyover with its massed tanks had featured so much on the TV news in June 1989, it now looked like Hong Kong in the early 60s. Every flat roof seemed to have a large neon advertising sign on it and there appeared to be more new buildings than old. Stepping into one department store you would have sworn you were in Hong Kong and there were two McDonalds in the area – mostly frequented thankfully by young Chinese rather than just foreigners. A very daring new venture of a coffee shop in the Friendship Store in the 80s, had transformed into a Pizza Hut and a French patisserie. Around the area of the Embassies there were quite a few foreign-looking bars and cafes, many of which seemed to be geared for Russian speakers.

The railway station, once so prominent on the skyline, still stood but much dwarfed and less busy since the building of a much larger new station further out of the city centre. It boasted an enormous TV screen on the front (to keep the crowds amused?) but still, thank goodness, bravely chimed out 'The East Is Red' every hour. Walking around the station area, just one block from the modernity, I was relieved to see the hutongs, the tricycles delivering coal briquettes and the warm welcoming glow of the restaurants along the street serving Mongolian Hot Pot, and on the pavement the roaring concrete stoves and bubbling woks and delicious smells. (I wasn't so keen on the miserable looking chickens in cages awaiting the next diners). Still there too, were the low hanging wires and metal poles and holes in the pavement so hazardous in the very dim lighting – the 40 watt light bulb still reigned supreme!

Many of the shops and food markets had been replaced, often by rather costly jewellery and clothing stores which seemed devoid of customers. Far fewer people seemed to frequent the, now more permanent, free markets which made the dirty beggars and their children more obtrusive. Remembering the rotten apples and walls of cabbages it was amazing to see so much fruit on sale in January, mostly coming from the south of China. Bananas, pears, kiwi fruit and even strawberries were displayed. Not all of this exotic produce was shipped in by shops or large markets: entrepreneurs travelled independently to Hainan and brought back as much as they could to sell on their private stalls. (Air and train travel had become much easier and it was even possible to book in advance!) I did see one small load of cabbages, in a hutong; apparently young people didn't bother with it any more and only the older generation still stored it up for the winter months. Not only was there a much greater choice, but young people could afford to buy the more expensive items.

The 'old' Friendship Store hadn't changed one bit, but there was a new one opened to the north, in the Lufthansa Centre. There were electronic tills, foreign clothes as well as Chinese, and small 'boutique' franchises with electronic tagging devices. The foreign clothes were a bargain, as they were not imported but made in China for overseas companies, and could be sold much cheaper in Beijing, and there were a lot of very smartly dressed young Chinese ladies around. The old wrapping paper that tore even as you folded it had been replaced with decorated foil, and there were even gift wrapping desks. For some reason, no matter how modern the shops might have been the toilets were still as awful and smelly as ever and you still got wet feet when you flushed them.

Even the truly 'locals' shop, the Bai Huo Da Lou in Wangfujing had done away with its displays of string, zips, buttons and webbing and replaced them with makeup, electric woks, microwaves, food processors and electric massagers. On the street outside it was still possible to buy a newspaper off a vendor, but there were new magazines and calendars showing Mr. Universe/Gladiators type men and women, the like of which would never have been allowed before.

Less cycling, more sitting and the health problems related to lack of exercise had just started to rear their ugly heads. As awareness of this grew so too did the opening of health clubs, and the humorists had a field day suggesting that instead of paying a lot of money to ride an exercise bike one could always ride a real bike to work – that was free.

Apart from the great increase in the number of cars and the greater affluence of many people, the most audible change was in the incredible number of mobile phones. When one of our artist friends had got a telephone pager he had really hit the heights, but six years on and everywhere you went someone was standing talking on a mobile phone or being summoned by an insistent bleeper.

Some things' demise I regretted: smart and modern though the hotels were, there had been a certain atmosphere about the ropey plumbing, and the enormous thermos flasks of boiling water and glass of tea leaves did have something that a Philips kettle, china cups and sealed packets of coffee, tea and creamer lacked. Disposable chopsticks in sealed packets had arrived too. The fish pond in the Beijing Hotel coffee shop, downfall of many an inebriated foreigner, was no more. Plastic strips had replaced the heavy, padded leather door curtains so effective in keeping winter draughts out of shops. The Amenities Hall at the British Embassy had been converted into office space, and the final threat to abolish F.E.C had been carried out, which saw an end to the instant and automatic lowering of prices in the clothes markets.

There had been some quite giant 'leaps forward' and some much smaller ones: hard hats were worn by the majority of people on building sites, padded split-crotched trousers were still worn but with disposable nappies underneath and helping to ease the transportation crush a few double-decker buses had been brought into service (often brightly painted and sporting advertising logos).

At the time of our return visit Chinese television was running a series on the life of Deng Xiao Ping, and one young man we met commented that he admired Deng and considered him to be a great leader of his time. He also spoke openly of the uprising in June 1989, a subject totally taboo before, and said he considered that, in retrospect, it had been a good thing that the students and workers had not succeeded. When asked why, he explained that there had been no real workable alternative to the government of the time and had it been overthrown, he thought that China would most likely have fallen apart like Russia did. Having had no time to track down more than a few old friends I could not tell whether his views were generally held by the younger generation. Were they content with the new affluence and greater freedoms, or would they once again 'rise up' one day, and if they did would it be as easy to stop them:

they had seen much greater freedom than in 1989 and might well fight harder to keep and enlarge it. I just do not know the answer to all those questions, but I hope that the continued changes will be for the better – of all. Perhaps I shall return in the year 2001 to see - it will then be 12 years since 1989, and the Chinese always used to believe in 12 year cycles.

Chapter Sixteen: A Few of My Favourite Places

Beijing ('Northern Capital') had so many fascinating sights, both large and small and time never seemed long enough, but I had a few definite favourites.

Tian An Men Square

We'd seen photos of it but only by standing there could you really feel the vastness of what is said to be the largest square in the world. To the north was the outer gateway leading to the Forbidden City, with Chairman Mao's portrait staring out over the square. High above him on the gateway hung the national emblem, depicting the gateway itself, symbol of modern China; a cogwheel to represent the workers; ears of grain for the peasants; five stars to symbolise the solidarity of the various nationalities of the Country and the colour red standing for the spirit of the revolution. To the west of the square stood the Great Hall of the People, boasting the most enormous columns, and on the opposite, east, side its near mirror-image, the Museums of History and of the Revolution. The size of the Great Hall was all the more amazing when you realised that the banquet hall alone could hold five thousand guests for a dinner and twice that number for a cocktail party. There were also thirty smaller halls, each one representing a particular province, and decorated in a style typical of that area. This building, opened in 1959, took just 10 months to complete as it had to be opened in time to mark the 10th Anniversary of the founding of the People's Republic of China. Such a vast open space as Tian An Men Square could hardly be dominated by any building or edifice erected in the centre, even the tallest monument in China: the Monument to the People's Heroes. It was carved with inscriptions and calligraphy of Chairman Mao and Zhou Enlai, together with representations of symbolic flowers: peony for nobility, lotus for purity and chrysanthemum for perseverance. Carved on marble were scenes from Chinese history, from the Opium War through various uprisings to Sun Yat-sen's revolution of 1911, the war against Japan and the victories of the People's Liberation Army in 1949. Just to the south of the Monument was the Mausoleum of the great leader himself, open to the public for some hours every day: a hushed, slow-moving queue gently shuffled around the square building prepared to wait for some hours for a glimpse of Chairman Mao. Glimpse it was, as you were not allowed to stop inside the building, but had to keep moving through the anterooms to the hall where the body lay. Some said it was only a waxwork, the original having been replaced after an ear fell off one night, nearly giving the guard on duty a heart attack! Whatever the truth, there was an indescribable, hushed atmosphere inside. Outside the Mausoleum was one of the few patches of colour in the square, apart from kites, provided by small trees and shrubs from all the regions of China. Even they contained an element of symbolism, there being thirteen pines from the north west as Mao spent thirteen years there.

Tian An Men Square was originally a part of the Forbidden City itself, but later cut off by the main road passing through it. The only indication left of its previous situation was the fact that the renovated gateway to the south of the square still bore the name 'Qianmen' or Front Gate.

The Forbidden City

- also once called the Purple Forbidden City, purple being the colour associated with the North Star, the centre of the universe. (The Chinese name for their Country means 'Middle Kingdom' and is placed at the centre of world maps, so the Emperor resided at the centre of the centre). Until 1911 no member of the public was allowed access to the City, as it was both an Imperial residence and the administrative centre of China.

Before entering what became the front gate you passed two enormous marble lions placed on either side of the roadway. Always found in pairs, the female rested one front paw on a playful cub, whilst the male had a ball beneath one of his upraised ones, the ball being either a pearl or the world (depending on who's telling the story). As you looked towards any doorway or gateway the female lion is on the left, male on the right. Next to the lions were tall marble pillars carved with dragons and rather stylised clouds at the top. In ancient times a leader would erect a wooden pillar and any complaints or criticisms could be carved on it by the people. Later the pillars were used to mark boundaries and as sign posts, but finally became purely ornamental. Atop the pillars of the Forbidden City were carved mythical creatures, but not all were facing the same direction: it was because those facing south were to watch and report on the Emperor's behaviour whenever he left the Palace, and those facing north had to watch his conduct inside the Imperial City itself. Five small, arched bridges spanned the moat that surrounded the Forbidden City with its unmistakeable vermilion walls and yellow roof tiles, both of which colours were reserved for the Emperor's sole use.

A long walk through gateways and across more tiny bridges led you finally to the main buildings: all built in a straight line and each facing south. The first few halls were used for meeting officials and conducting state business (and boasted some fine, elevated thrones and ornate incense burners), the middle section was reserved for the Emperor and his wives, and the north part consisted of a garden for quiet relaxation. Within the garden were small pavilions, and rocks specially chosen for their aesthetic value. Even the pathways had tiny pebbles inlaid in them in the shapes of animals, birds and flowers. Each building was separated from the rest by a large courtyard, and was raised up above ground level. Access for the Emperor was by being carried in a sedan chair over a carved marble slope (the 'dragon pavement'), the mere mortals of this world having to toil up steps on either side: only the Emperor was allowed up the central slope or in by the central door.

Because of their size the halls must have been very cool in summer, but bitterly cold in winter. A large portion of each wall was made of wooden latticed window frames which were left empty in the summer to allow free flow of air, but in the colder months thin paper was pasted over the frames to afford some sort of protection. Paper was also used in the same way to afford privacy, although a wet finger rubbed over it made a small hole through which the curious could peep, if they dared. With the almost exclusive use of wood in the buildings, fire was a constant worry, so large cauldrons of water were kept to hand, with fires lit under them in winter to prevent the water freezing. One particularly fine pair of gold-covered bronze cauldrons still bore the scratched marks inflicted by the allied troops' bayonets when they entered the Palace in 1900 and tried to scrape off the gold.

Apart from the large, impressive halls there were an enormous number of smaller rooms and courtyards once occupied by concubines, eunuchs and servants, some of which had been set up with displays of jewellery or refurnished as they would have been when originally occupied, with beautifully carved kangs adorned with silk drapes and cushions, and even the makeup boxes of the concubines. Every girl's name was written on a bamboo strip, one of which the Emperor would pick at random. A eunuch would then be dispatched to fetch the chosen concubine: he would wrap her, naked, in a silken rug and carry her to the Imperial presence where the rug would be unrolled and she would fall at his feet. Being a concubine in the Forbidden City was a much sought after position, bringing not only security in your own life but prestige and favour to your entire family; provided of course that you did not incur the wrath of others senior to yourself — even the Empress Dowager was not above pushing a favourite concubine down a well. For a man too, employment in the Imperial Court was to be envied, bringing wealth and often power, especially if you found favour with the Emperor, and a good income from bribery and corruption. The price paid was high too, for you had to prove yourself to be a eunuch by providing your severed parts for inspection. These would be kept in the Palace (so you couldn't lend them to anyone who wanted to cheat the system) and only returned to you in great old age so that you could be buried 'intact'. For all those who were accepted into the Palace employ, many must have died a painful death from the terrible infections caused by the totally barbaric operation and insanitary equipment used to perform it.

In one of the halls there was also a sizeable exhibition of clocks: the Empress Dowager Cixi had a passion for them and anyone wanting to curry favour would present her with yet another. They ranged from small and bejewelled to large and mechanised, from beautiful to downright hideous!

The Hall of Imperial Longevity housed portraits of the Imperial ancestors, and the View of Virtue Hall was used first for archery practice and then as a resting place for dead Emperors prior to their burial outside the city.

Across the entrances to all halls and courtyards were the customary sills to prevent the passage of evil spirits, except strangely in one long passageway: the story was that they had all been removed to allow the young, and last, Emperor Puyi to ride his bicycle.

The northern exit from the garden was through yet another large gateway which at one time housed drums and bells. In the past the bells would toll one hundred and eight times (12 x 9) at dusk and again at dawn, with the drums sounding out the watches of the night. Presumably the Emperor slept far enough away that he wasn't disturbed by them. The original Imperial City continued across the road and the moat to include the renamed Jingshan Park. There was originally a small grassy hillock called Green Hill onto which was built an artificial, tree-covered hill called the Jingshan. Its purpose was to improve the feng shui of the Palace (balance of wind and water so vital to its occupants) and to protect the buildings from evil. When the moat was dug at a later date, the earth was dumped at this most northerly point of the City and formed into five peaks instead of the original one, each eventually topped with a small pavilion. Yet further in its history coal was stored there, giving it the alternative name of Coal Hill Park. A rather mundane park, but one steeped in history: the pavilions had housed bronze statues of gods, but they were mostly stolen by the light-fingered allied troops. In 1644, as a result of a peasants' uprising, the last Ming Emperor hanged himself here from a locust tree.

Looking down on the sea of golden roofs of the Forbidden City one small, almost square building stands out because of its extremely ornate dragons undulating along the ridges. All the other buildings have rows of ceramic creatures in a line along the lower part of each ridge. The story behind them is that one particular bad ruler was punished by being tied to a chicken and sent out onto the furthest point of the roof with fierce animals lined up behind them. The man was too scared to return past the animals and the chicken was too scared to jump off the roof, so there they all stayed, marooned forever. The Forbidden City was built rather uniformly, the halls only really differing in size rather than design; the exception being the four corner towers, whose building was instigated by the Emperor Yongle. He decided that the towers should have nine beams, eighteen pillars and seventy two roof ridges – and if the architect and builders couldn't achieve it within three months they'd all be executed. As time passed and they'd come up with no plans, they spent the days wracking their brains and the nights unable to sleep for the worry and the increasing heat of summer. One of the carpenters decided to spend the hot evenings walking through the streets to enjoy his last weeks before losing his head. One evening he heard a pedlar selling crickets, which supposedly brought good luck and, needing all the luck he could get, he bought one in a very ornate straw cage. His colleagues were none too impressed with his wasting his time wandering around the streets while they desperately tried to come up with some plan to appease the Emperor and save their lives, until one of them noticed the cricket cage: there it was, nine beams, eighteen pillars and seventy two roof ridges – all they had to do was transfer the whole from millet stalks to wood and tiles.

To the west of the Forbidden City and once a part of it, were the North, Middle and South Seas (large lakes), whose Chinese names were Bei Hai, Zhong Hai and Nan Hai. The Middle and South Seas were combined into Zhongnan Hai, and kept for the exclusive use, both residential and business, of the top Communist leaders. The North Sea was opened to the public as Beihai Park, little different from many of the others around the city except for one large and unmistakeable landmark – the white Dagoba. The almost bottle-shaped 'building', Tibetan in style, was erected to commemorate the Dalai Lama's visit to Beijing in 1652 and the base was covered in tiny carved Buddhas, showing some signs of having been defaced during the Cultural Revolution. The park also boasted the fine 'Nine Dragon Screen' made of brightly coloured ceramic tiles with raised dragons on, and a smaller screen resembling iron but made of volcanic rock, which was erected in memory of two unusually kind dragons who tried to rid Beijing of the dust storms brought about by the wicked Wind Witch and Cloud Boy. Easy to miss would be the Round City, a small walled-off section of the park with its own entrance, from which slightly elevated position the Court could enjoy a view over the gardens and lake. I was less interested in the view than in the two pieces of jade housed there. The first was a very large wine bowl carved from a single piece of black jade and used by the Kublai Khan, the second a peaceful Buddha statue carved from white jade and bearing a slight scratch on one arm inflicted by those allied troops again.

Summer Palace

Without the modern invention of air-conditioners, summer in Beijing was uncomfortably hot, so the Emperor and Court would retreat to the Park of Nurtured Harmony, or Summer Palace. From its earliest days as a small hill and pond it was developed into part of a massive complex of three hills and five parks, but in the 1800s the foreigners invaded and destroyed the majority of the buildings. When the fierce and infamous Cixi (who hardly took after her name, which means 'Compassionate Fortune') became Empress Dowager, one of the Princes tried to curry favour with her by restoring the park, but to avoid criticism of spending vast amounts of money, he said he was setting up a Naval Academy. After ten years (in 1895) the work was complete and the beautiful park certainly pleased Cixi – it was reputed to be her favourite place. In 1900 the foreigners struck again, but once they'd been dispatched she allocated herself an enormous sum of money to repair the damage, money reportedly earmarked for improvements to, and modernisation of, the Navy. Unfortunately completion of the work didn't mean much of a lessening of the amount of the Country's money being spent, for when the Empress Dowager was in a spending mood there was no stopping her. She took more than 1,200 eunuchs and attendants with her for the summer, 123 of which were cooks to prepare her food alone. She loved theatre and had one built there, spending a fortune on props and actors. The theatre, as all old Chinese ones, was open-air and without curtains. It had three storeys, the top floor being for immortals, the middle one for humans and the lowest one for the devil. It was also the only Palace to be lit by electricity rather than candles.

The focal point of the acres of park, gardens and buildings was undoubtedly Longevity Hill with Kunming Lake at its foot, but not to be passed by unnoticed was the Painted Corridor, a long covered walkway with four octagonal pavilions spaced out along its length. Every ceiling, crossbeam and available flat surface was painted with vivid scenes of landscapes, battles, stories from literature, birds or flowers: to me it was the most unusual and interesting art gallery in the world. Apparently the artists employed to produce these works never sketched a design first, they just painted freehand. If the Empress Dowager did misappropriate the funds for the Navy at least she had one boat built, albeit a marble one, two-storey with stained glass windows and firmly attached to dry land.

At the 'back' of the Palace grounds was a complex of buildings appearing totally out of context amongst all the Chinese style of architecture, as they replicated Tibetan temples. One of the small halls in the area apparently afforded a view outside the walls, and from there Cixi was said to watch the common people going to market. Wanting to see what it was like to be a commoner, she had a row of shops built inside the Palace walls by the side of the Back Lake where she could 'buy' things from the eunuchs dressed as shop keepers, and mingle with 'the people' – actually eunuchs and servants in disguise.

The nearby Park of Perfection and Brightness was also called the Old Summer Palace and was really little more than a pile of ruins (those foreigners again). There was talk of an attempt to restore it to its former 'glory', but if the artist's impression was anything to go by, it would be best left well alone! It appeared to have been largely influenced by

Jesuits attached to the Qing Court, but Renaissance-looking architecture just didn't seem right in the north of China.

Temple of Heaven

Every year the Emperor would go to the Temple of Heaven to worship heaven and to pray for good harvests. I wonder if he found the main hall of the temple as breathtaking as we did: raised up on three marble terraces, the circular building had a triple roof tiled with the deep blue colour reserved for religious buildings, and the sky behind always seemed to be blue too. The ceiling inside was intricately and ornately painted and carved with dragons (the Emperor) and phoenixes (the Empress) and a marble slab set into the middle of the floor bore natural veining also resembling dragon and phoenix (a bit of artistic licence there, I thought. It could have represented just about anything you chose.) In the whole building not a single nail, piece of metal or concrete was used, the whole being kept together with interlocking wooden beams, brackets and joints. As if the sheer beauty of the design were not enough, symbolic numbers had to be incorporated into the plans: there were 28 pillars for the constellations, of which the 4 central ones stood for the seasons, the next 12 for the months of the lunar calendar and a further 12 were to represent the number of two-hour periods into which day and night were traditionally divided. In addition, if you added the two 12s together, you had the 24 solar periods in a year.

Having prayed, the Emperor would progress along a long, raised marble causeway to another, smaller circular building which housed the memorial tablet of the 'Ruler of Heaven'. The interesting thing about this part of the complex wasn't the building, but the wall around it, the Echo Wall: circular and with a peculiar property that if you whispered at one point of it your message could be heard clearly at the point opposite.

The final part of the group of temple buildings (the largest such group in China) was a large, three tiered marble altar, open to the elements. Again, symbolism was all important: the outer wall was square to represent the earth ('4 corners'), the inner one round, for heaven. The total number of balustrades was 360 – the number of degrees in a circle. The central flagstone of the altar was surrounded by a circle of 9 stones, the next circle outside that had 18, and so on in multiples of 9 until the outer, ninth, circle which had 81 stones. Even the flights of steps were in groups of 9.

The few souvenir shops found around the temple area had originally sold herbal medicine for women, made from the motherwort plants which used to grow on the site. They were not native to the area but had been planted there by a young and devoted daughter, who had travelled for many days to find a cure for her dying mother. When the Temple of Heaven was built, the Emperor was alarmed at the state of the courtyards which were covered in 'weeds', and demanded they be cleared. Both the wife and mother of one of the Court Ministers took the motherwort medicine regularly and knew the plant could not be found anywhere else, so he came up with an ingenious idea. He persuaded the Emperor that the plant was called 'dragonbeard' and had magical properties – the Emperor was after all a dragon, and he did want to grow a beard...the motherwort was spared.

The Temple of Heaven was for the Emperor's use, but there were many other temples at which common people could pray and worship, of which two, to my mind, stood out above the rest.

Lama Temple

Erected in 1694, the original buildings on this site were the palace of a Manchu Prince, the fourth son of the Emperor Kang Xi. The eldest son was disinherited as being unfit to become Emperor, and the 'Mandate of Heaven' was passed to this fourth son who quickly dispatched any rivals and became Emperor Yong Zheng. He then moved into the Forbidden City itself, but declared his old home to be an 'Imperial Travelling Residence' and therefore forbidden to commoners. He had all the green roof tiles removed and replaced with Imperial yellow ones and renamed it Palace of Harmony. Presumably it was too near home to be used much as a travelling residence, so he later gave it to Lamaist monks to use. When a member of the Imperial family died his or her former home could not revert to common use, but had to be turned into a temple and as the Lamas were already in residence in the Palace of Harmony it naturally became their temple upon Yong Zheng's death.

Although open to the public as a tourist site, the Lama Temple was an active one with resident monks and young novices. As with all temples there were the customary bell and drum towers and various halls dedicated to the study of mathematics, astronomy, medicine and 'esoteric scriptures'. In one, there were also two rather incongruous models of bears in remembrance of the bears once caught by the Emperor Qianlong on a hunting trip. There was also a beautiful bronze model of Mount Sumeru (the centre of the world to Buddhists) with inscriptions in Han, Manchu, Mongolian and Tibetan, but it was in the last two halls that the real delights were to be found. The Hall of the Wheel of the Law was dominated by a statue of Tsongkhapa, a great religious reformer who wanted Lamaism (Tibetan Buddhism) to return to its pure form and so started a breakaway sect, The Yellow Sect, who donned yellow robes as opposed to red. There were colourful and fascinating murals showing Sakyamuni on his missionary travels and, being a 'working' temple, along the walls were racks containing three hundred and fifteen important works of scripture and mats laid out in front of low tables before the statue in readiness for the monks' next religious ceremony. As you left the Hall, the door being behind the wall backing on to the statue, a backward glance revealed yet another treasure, a wonderfully and intricately carved representation of the Mountain of Five Hundred Arhats carved out of red sandalwood, the five hundred tiny figures made of gold, silver, bronze, iron or tin.

The final Pavilion of Ten Thousand Happinesses was ten thousand times more impressive than any temple building I had ever seen. The central three storey tower was flanked on either side by two storey pavilions which were joined to the tower by covered bridges. The first time I saw this Hall was prior to its renovation, and I must confess I preferred it in its more dilapidated state as it seemed to have more atmosphere and didn't just look like every other repainted temple. Inside, gallery rails were missing, paint was peeling, cobwebs hung high in the rafters and the air smelt musty, but all paled into insignificance beside the enormous statue of Maitreya, hand raised in blessing, a totally peaceful expression on its face. You had to crane your neck to look up at the head, which was given the most ethereal atmosphere as the sun filtered through the windows, cobwebs and dust at the top of the tower. The wonderful statue was carved from the single trunk of a dragon spruce which was sent to Beijing as a gift from the 7th Dalai Lama (it took three years in transit), and stood eighteen metres high with a further eight metres buried under the ground. When a gown was made for it, one thousand seven hundred and ninety nine metres of material were needed. Facts and figures aside, nothing I saw in Beijing left quite such an impression on me.

The Temple of Azure Clouds and the Temple of the Sleeping Buddha

Situated outside the city, on the east of the Western Hills, the Temple of Azure Clouds was first built as a convent, and being built on a hill was on six different levels. It was enlarged over the years, and the impressive marble pagoda was modelled on the one in Bihar in India to commemorate Sakyamuni's attainment of Buddhahood. In 1929 Sun Yat-sen died in Beijing and his coffin was placed in this pagoda before its removal to Nanjing: his clothes and hat were said to be sealed inside still. In a courtyard way off to one side was to be found the most unusual collection of statues, in the Hall of Five Hundred Arhats. Arhats were divine beings (but of lesser standing than Buddhas and Bodhisattvas) who were given the job of preaching Buddhist doctrines on earth. Each of the five hundred Arhat statues in the Hall was numbered and each had a different expression and pose but were all the same size and colour. The building was in the shape of a cross, each of the four 'arms' housing rows of them and with seven additional deities standing in the passageways. There was even a very junior monk squatting up on a roof beam - the story was that he arrived late and had nowhere to sit. Had these fascinating Arhats been displayed in a museum, under good lighting they would have been just a collection of statues, but in the dimly lit temple building they took on an almost dreamlike quality and you would hardly have been surprised had one of them spoken to you.

Not far from the Azure Clouds was a temple housing a fifty four ton, over five metres high Buddha, except that he wasn't as much 'high' as 'long', as he was the Sleeping or Recumbent Buddha. There had been a temple and Sleeping Buddha on the site since the 7th Century, although both statue and buildings had been replaced and rebuilt many times. Behind the statue stood twelve disciples, the whole scene a re-enactment of the time when Sakyamuni, knowing he was soon to leave them, issued instructions to his followers whilst resting under the shade of a tree. He certainly looked very relaxed and comfortable – he had even taken his shoes off, and around the walls of the hall were display cases containing embroidered cloth shoes presented to this statue by the Qing Emperors.

There were many, many temples to be visited in Beijing; many rather similar so that one blended into another in the memory, but one housed a unique collection of bells including the largest one in China (six and a half metres high and weighing forty six tons). There were two impressive things about that particular bell: firstly, its whole surface was covered with hundreds of thousands of characters of religious text, and secondly, the ingenious method used to move it there from its original position on the city walls. Long before the days of cranes and heavy-duty vehicles the Chinese often moved very heavy objects long distances simply by taking advantage of their climate. Once winter arrived the tracks from the bell's original home to the temple were frozen, making it a comparatively easy task to slide it along. To raise it up onto the enormous frame made for it also made use of the sub-zero temperatures: a mound of earth was piled up under the frame and then covered in water until it froze into an 'ice mountain'. By using ropes and a lot of muscle, the enormous bell slid up the slope and was firmly mounted in its final position, the earth mound then being removed.

Liulichang

Although many of the fine old buildings in the city were preserved, they were dotted about all over the place so gave you no real impression of 'old' Beijing. There was one place however, where a whole street of shops was renovated, giving you the chance to step back in time away from the modern world (except for the tourists, of course).

In the early Ming Dynasty a special factory, called Liulichang, was established to produce glazed pottery for the Imperial Court, but in the early Qing Dynasty the smoke from the factory was thought to be in danger of polluting the Palace so the factory was relocated. Later the area became a residential site with many guild halls and hostels, the latter being built by Court officials for students from their home provinces who came to Beijing to sit the government examinations (success in which entitled you to a junior civil servant post). Because of the number of students in the area, bookshops began to open up, selling not only books but calligraphy equipment as well. Some of the shopkeepers became informal tutors to their customers, and at one stage of its history Liulichang was supposed to be the gathering place of witchdoctors.

Totally renovated, Liulichang had reopened as a centre for bookshops, painting and calligraphy and antiques, and one of the best places to buy the 'four treasures of the study' (writing brushes, ink slabs, ink sticks and fine paper) revered by all scholars. The Studio of Glorious Treasures also specialised in the art of woodblock printing, a craft dating back over one thousand years. A 'master' painting was traced out onto transparent paper, one sheet for every colour in the original, and each sheet was then pasted onto a separate block of wood which was carved to the exact design. Applying one colour to each of the blocks and carefully printing them one on top of the other onto paper, gave you a bright, if laborious to produce, picture. An interesting aside: in the past, paintings in China were not valued for sale by their beauty or desirability, but by their size.

The City Walls

Almost all of Beijing's Manchu city wall was demolished and the stones used to build the Underground Train tunnels, which one might think was only a loss to the visual beauty of Beijing, but along with their demolition went a part of the city's history, for many of the ornate and impressive gateways were more than just doors through the defences, but had special parts to play in the everyday workings of the city. The Gate of the Rising Sun (Chaoyangmen) was where tribute rice from the south of China arrived by canal and was stored in huge buildings inside the gate. The Due East Gate (Dongzhimen) was where wood was unloaded from the canal, whereas the Gate of Peace (Andingmen) was the passage of nightsoil out to the sewage farms, and the passage of returning armies back into the city. The only gate still standing was the Gate of Virtue and Victory (Deshengmen) through which armies left on their campaigns. Water from the Jade Spring, for use at the Emperor's table, came in through the Due West Gate (Xizhimen) and coal through the Gate of Abundance (Fuchengmen). In 1495 an elephant stables was built at the Renaissance Gate (Fuxingmen). The elephants were a present from Burma and were used in ceremonies and to pull the Emperor's carriage when he went to sacrifice at the Temple of Heaven. Unfortunately no one had any real idea of how to care for them, and by 1860 all elephants had died out. In 1873 more elephants arrived from Burma and on the 6th day of the 6th month every year they were ceremonially washed in the moat, but in 1884 one went berserk and injured a passerby, so the elephants were never brought out or used again, nor were they replaced when the last one died. In the early 1900s a parliamentary building was sited there. One gate feared by all was that of Majesty of Arms (Xuanwumen) as those who left from there were to be executed in the vegetable market in the southern city. The two towers of the Gate Which Faces the Sun (Qianmen) still stood, but long gone were the walls and courtyards and the temples to Guan Di the god of war, and Guan Yin, a goddess who showed such compassion that even as she reached the gates of heaven she felt compelled to return to earth because she heard a baby cry. The Gate of Sublime Learning (Chongwenmen) would have been a popular gate as wine entered the city there.

There were two other interesting places along the wall's length, one being the site of the Palace of the Fourth Prince. Towards the end of the 17th Century prisoners taken at the Siege of Albazin were kept there, most being Russians. With them was a priest, Maxim Leontiew, who converted a small pagoda into a church dedicated to Saint Nicholas. In 1900 the whole place was sacked, but thereafter gradually rebuilt until, in 1949, the church was once again destroyed and the land handed over to the Soviet Embassy to develop into its new (and still existent) compound. The second building was the Observatory, dating from 1280, on which roof was a wonderful collection of old astrological instruments, and inside, displays, charts and a wealth of information – in Chinese. As far as I could gather, Chinese astronomers had observed 'Halley's' comet 2,500 years before Halley did, eclipses were recorded 4,000 years ago, sunspots were discovered 16 centuries before Galileo and many stellar and lunar charts were first drawn up here. In the small shop it was possible to buy feng shui compasses and reproductions of the earliest type of compass which had a spoon-shaped pointer, which seemed to point south.

Sadly long gone, but which would have been an amazing sight were it still standing, was the mysterious Fox Tower. No one seemed to know its original purpose, but it was carefully measured to stand ninety nine feet high and no more, as good spirits soared through the air at one hundred feet and nothing should impede them. I would also love to have been able to view the Imperial Examination Grounds, built under the Ming Emperor Yong Le. All the important exams were held every three years, the successful candidates earning the title 'Doctor' and a chance to get on in life. Candidates had first to change into special clothes, to avoid concealment of helpful 'cribs' and were then locked into one of the eight thousand five hundred small narrow cells, whose doors were sealed for the three days and nights of the exam. Imperial Examinations were discontinued in 1900 and the buildings pulled down in 1913.

The Great Wall (or 10,000 'Li' Long Wall)

"If you haven't climbed the Great Wall you can't call yourself a man" the saying went. Surely no one could have failed to hear about this mighty creation, visible from the moon, so it was with great anticipation that I first approached the Eight Prominent Peaks (Badaling), the section of Wall open to the public. Awful confession that it might be, but my first emotion was one of disappointment; I think I had expected to see a gigantic wall towering over us all, blotting out the sun, but it wasn't really very high at all, just sections of crenellated wall with two storey watchtowers situated at intervals along its length. Having climbed onto the Wall itself however, I was impressed: it was not the height or width that took one's breath away, but the sheer vastness, the length of it. For as far as the eye could see it snaked away into the grey, misty distance and you could imagine it stretching across the whole of the vastness of China. Standing on the watchtowers you could imagine the soldiers of history grateful for the shade provided against the burning sun of summer, or huddled round open fires in the bitter winters; and then you would think of the misery of the hundreds of thousands of conscripted labourers and convicts who had had to build it. They were afforded no such shelter and thousands died and were said to have been buried in the Wall itself. The total workforce was said to have been nearly a million: about a fifth of the total workforce of the whole of China at that time. It was never built as one long wall in fact, but a series of shorter disconnected ones, finally joined together by order of Emperor Qin Shi, which accounted for the fact that some sections were so wide that six horses could be driven abreast whilst others were narrow and winding. It snaked along the top of ranges of hills, giving great changes in gradient too; some parts were gentle slopes, others very steep and with uneven steps making both ascent and descent exhausting, and it was not unusual to see elderly Chinese ladies, fulfilling a lifetime's ambition of climbing the Wall, having to sit down and slide down steep slopes whose paving stones had been worn as smooth as ice by the feet of thousands. One of the principal ingredients of the mortar used in the Wall was glutinous (or 'sticky') rice, but I did discover one section that was made of painted polystyrene! Not the usual way of repairs, but specially designed to crumble dramatically during the making of a film.

Equally impressive, although much further away, was the eastern end of the Great Wall, where you could see it literally tumbling into the sea. This dramatic area was called the Pass Between Mountain and Sea (Shanhaiguan) and the nearby city gate was named The First Gate Under Heaven. Nearby was a temple dedicated to a faithful wife, Meng Jiang Nu. She was a beautiful girl who lived happily with her husband until the Emperor's soldiers arrived in the village and took all the strong young men away to work on the construction of the Great Wall. Unable to bear her loneliness and worry, she eventually trekked for days to reach the place where he had been sent, only to find that her husband was already dead. In her misery she banged her head against the brickwork and the Wall, feeling for her pain, cracked open to reveal his body. She arranged to take the body home for burial, but by that time the Emperor himself had seen her and fallen in love with her (or so he said!) He wanted her as a concubine and, rather uncharacteristically, wanted her to go to him willingly rather than by force. Knowing that she had no choice in the matter she asked if first a memorial to her husband could be erected – a small platform in the sea. That was done, and before moving into the Palace she asked permission to stand on the memorial platform and bid her husband farewell. As she stood there she turned to the Emperor and told him that true love could only remain faithful to one person, whether dead or alive, and as he had in effect killed the husband he would never have the wife – and she threw herself into the sea and drowned.

The Ming Tombs (or the Thirteen Tombs)

The thirteen tombs of the Ming Dynasty were dotted around the lower slopes of rolling hills to the north west of Beijing. Long before the actual burial mounds, you passed a large marble archway with six columns and five arches, elaborately decorated with carvings of animals, dragons and clouds. This marked the start of the Sacred Way (also called the Road to Immortality), a road some seven or more kilometres long along which the bodies of the dead Emperors were carried to their final resting places. Further along, the Great Palace Gate straddled the road; a gateway of three arches, the middle one of which was reserved for the Emperor's body, and no living person was ever to pass through it. Another short distance and you arrived at a building housing an enormous stone tortoise with a tall stone pillar (a stele) on its back which was carved with the calligraphy of two of the Emperors. More impressive by far than those buildings were the statues on either side of the next section of the Sacred Way, each carved from a single piece of white marble. First were two lions standing facing each other, one on either side of the road, followed by two kneeling lions. Next came xiezhai (mythical beasts), camels, elephants, qilin (mythical) and horses – two pairs of each, one pair always standing, one pair kneeling. The choice of creatures was far from arbitrary: the mythical beasts were there to attack intruders and to signify the dignity of the place, and the other animals were there to work. Artistic licence combined with practicality when it came to the kneeling elephants, as the front legs bent the wrong way at the knees so the statues didn't overbalance. Beyond the animals were larger than life-sized men, four each of officials, generals and ministers, but unlike their animal companions these were all standing, although sunk several inches down into the earth. There was a story that each of these statues had some imperfection or piece missing that was not so when they were first sited at the tombs. Apparently they all got rather bored guarding tombs day after day so at night they would get together for company. That soon palled too so they started going off to the villages looking for girls to talk to. One night one of the generals was spotted and had to run back to the tombs hell for leather, but tripped and chipped a piece of stone from his nose. Some time later the Emperor Qian Long wanted to move the statues to grace the approach of his own tomb and those of the other Emperors of the Qing Dynasty, but specified that he only wanted those that were unblemished. Qian Long's Prime Minister felt sorry for the statues and wanted them to remain together where they were, but dared not disobey the order to move them, until the statues themselves suggested a solution. Accordingly the Prime Minister hired a gang of people to go late one night and slightly damage each statue; the Emperor saw that they were not perfect and lost interest in them. One final gateway – Dragon and Phoenix Gate – and the road then divided into approaches to each of the thirteen tombs. Although their building spanned more than two hundred years they were all of the same basic design: a stele on a tortoise's back, a gateway, a tall two storey tower and finally the grass covered mound under which was the underground 'palace' containing the coffin. In keeping with all Imperial residences the buildings had vermilion coloured walls and yellow roof tiles. Those built by the Emperors themselves before death were on a much grander scale than any erected after death by the succeeding generation, and three of them had brick pits containing the bodies of the Emperors' female servants and concubines who were forced to commit suicide to accompany their dead masters. (The practice was abolished by the sixth Ming Emperor). It was very confusing trying to work out exactly who was buried where as Emperors had three names – personal name, reign name and tomb name, so Emperor Zhu Di ruled under the name of Yongle and was buried in Changling!

The two grandest tombs had been renovated and opened to the public: the best preserved of the two boasted a splendid, richly decorated entrance hall with pillars made of special wood which took over five years to reach Beijing from the mountains of south west China. Of the other tomb little of special interest remained above ground, but the underground chambers had been opened up. Flight after flight of stone steps led down the twenty seven metres to the complex of five halls with stone vaulted ceilings. Doorways were carved of marble and the floor bricks were specially made and fired and had taken years to produce. There were altars with incense burners and three marble daises for the coffins of the Emperor and his first and second wives. Many precious stones, jewels and ornaments were found when the chamber was excavated, including pieces of jade placed around the coffins to protect the bodies from decay, but had all since been removed to the safety of a museum. When the Emperor, whilst still young and fit, began work on his tomb the burial chambers were much more ornate, with wooden columns and beams all carved and painted. After twelve years' solid work they were near to completion when the builders learnt that they were to be executed lest they divulge the tomb's secrets. Hoping to save their necks (or rather, heads) they promptly burned the whole lot down. They won a reprieve from execution and were ordered to spend twelve more years building the tomb again. History repeated itself when, after that twelve years, the Emperor again mentioned execution and they again burned it to the ground. Taking good advice from one of his Ministers, the Emperor finally changed the plans and had a stone tomb. Presumably the masons and workers involved were executed once their work was done – not that they'd had a particularly easy time of it during construction: the enormous slabs of stone were too heavy to be transported from the quarry by any conventional means so wells were dug every half kilometre of the specially built route so that in winter water could be poured over the road to freeze into an ice path. Even dragging the blocks along on the ice could take thousands of men a month, from quarry to tomb.

The remaining eleven tombs seemed to be fast disintegrating into a state beyond repair: walls bulged and threatened to crash to earth at any moment, trees grew out of roofs and walls, but to me that was their attraction, dotted about amongst the trees, roofs just visible, they seemed far more in keeping with the peaceful surrounding hills than the brightly coloured, tourist filled ones.

There were, of course, many other places which I visited and will never forget. Tianjin (the Ford of Heaven), where the washbasin in the hotel emptied out onto the carpet at your feet, and the zoo had dogs and cats in cages as well as the more usual 'wild' animals. Xi'an, where the Terracotta Warriors defy description and had to be seen to be believed and where the local handicraft was wonderfully bright patchwork quilts and waistcoats. The tropical island of Hainan to the south, originally inhabited by aboriginal tribes and any undesirables banished from the mainland, with empty beaches on a par with those of Hawai'i, and where the best coffee and coconuts were grown but seldom seen for sale, as they were sold direct to the mainland. There you could buy a section of sugarcane to chew, extracting the sweet juice and spitting the woody residue out onto the ground. On a long bus journey from one part of the island to another a stop was made for all those needing to go to the toilet, the driver pointing to a clump of bushes on one side of the road for the ladies and a slightly smaller clump on the other side for the men! The baggage reclaim at the airport was only slightly more civilised: you stood on a stretch of tarmac while suitcases were literally tipped off the back of a lorry into a heap on the ground. In total contrast to the warmth of Hainan was the bitter cold of Harbin, way to the north, where was held every year the most wonderful display of ice carvings – from small models of animals, to statues, to mini Great Walls to large temples, and all made out of ice, some with coloured electric lights inside, some with real goldfish frozen inside as decoration. Water was sprayed onto trees and bushes which quickly froze into long icicles.

I shall always remember the people we met on our travels as well as the places, and one particular gentleman who started out slightly antagonistic and ended up as a friend. The name Yichang will be engraved on my heart, if not my liver, for it was at that particular city that more maotai was consumed than I care to remember. We were on an Attaché tour which included a river trip on the Yangzi and a tour of the Gezhouba Dam, a remarkable feat of engineering to tame the waters of the river, which had caused so many deaths and floods. We shared a table at the banquet with two other Attaché couples and the Manager of the building of the dam, who had little, if any, time for foreigners and intended to show it by drinking them under the table. As two of our fellow diners drank very little and the other two were Muslims, they naturally soon dropped out of the contest and left us to it. I hope no one ever counted the total number of 'ganbeis' we had to endure, but somewhere between the twenty fifth and thirtieth glass of maotai our Chinese host declared us to be "all right" after all and gave us one final toast, using a jam sandwich rather than liquor. Somehow we made it to the next morning's presentation on the building of the dam, and were glad to see our 'friend' didn't look any better than we felt, and he quickly handed over the talk to an assistant and came and sat quietly next to us. When it was time to walk round the mighty construction he signalled to us to wait behind and, once the rest had strode off in the wake of their guides, said that the three of us would have our own little tour at a sedate and restful pace as befitted those with mighty hangovers. The fresh air did us all good, and gazing down at the fury of the rushing waters below, Mike asked him if he'd ever had any doubts that the dam would hold when the first floods hit it. The official answer was instant – "No, we never doubted for a minute" – to be followed after the briefest of pauses by the quiet "Actually I slept in my office on site for three nights". Such total honesty showed we had not only won his respect, but had made a true friend.

35486482R00125

Printed in Great Britain
by Amazon